Teaching the Selected Works of Robert Cormier

The Young Adult Novels in the Classroom Series

When former Heinemann–Boynton/Cook editor Peter Stillman first conceived the Young Adult Literature (YAL) series in 1990 and asked me to be the series editor, I was excited to be part of such an innovative endeavor. At that time there were few professional books available for teachers who wanted to bring young adult literature into their classrooms, and Heinemann was the first publisher making a concerted effort to fill this need. Seventeen years and many books later, under the direction of Heinemann Executive Editor Lisa Luedeke, the series continues to inform and assist teachers at the middle school, high school, and college levels as they read with and teach to their students the best works that the field of young adult literature has to offer.

The Heinemann YAL Series takes another step forward with the book you hold in your hands. This subseries on teaching the works of specific young adult authors is designed to help you incorporate young adult literature into your curriculum, providing ideas and lessons that you may use and offering examples of classroom-tested student work, lesson plans, and discussion as an impetus to designing your own lessons and developing your own ideas in accordance with your students' needs.

The first two books in this series are *Teaching the Selected Works of Robert Cormier* and *Teaching the Selected Works of Mildred D. Taylor*. Next, Heinemann will publish books in 2007 that focus on the works of Katherine Paterson and Walter Dean Myers; later, books on teaching selected works of Chris Crutcher and Gary Paulsen will follow.

Over the years, many teachers in my graduate young adult literature classes have asked me how to convince administrators and parents that young adult literature is worthy of a place in the curriculum alongside the classics and other commonly taught literary works. In response I have shown them how to write rationales for specific books, how to design lesson plans and units that satisfy state and national standards, how to deal with censorship, and how to become connoisseurs of young adult literature themselves. I hope that the books in this subseries, by focusing on specific authors of young adult literature and highlighting the successful work of teachers with this genre, will inspire confidence in you to bring these extraordinary works into your curriculum, not just as a bridge to the classics, but as literary works in their own right.

—Virginia R. Monseau

Teaching the
Selected Works of
Robert Cormier

Virginia R. Monseau

HEINEMANN
PORTSMOUTH, NH

Heinemann
A division of Reed Elsevier Inc.
361 Hanover Street
Portsmouth, NH 03801–3912
www.heinemann.com

Offices and agents throughout the world

CIP data is on file at the Library of Congress.
ISBN-13: 978-0-325-00745-8
ISBN-10: 0-325-00745-4

Editor: Lisa Luedeke
Production: Vicki Kasabian
Cover design: Night & Day Design
Typesetter: Tom Allen, Pear Graphic Design
Manufacturing: Steve Bernier

Printed in the United States of America on acid-free paper
11 10 09 08 07 VP 1 2 3 4 5

To the memory of Robert Cormier

CONTENTS

Acknowledgments viii

Introduction: *Discovering Robert Cormier* ix

1 *After the First Death:* Dealing with the World as It Is 1

2 *Heroes:* What Does It Mean to Be Heroic? 23

3 *Tunes for Bears to Dance To:* The Destruction of Innocence 36

4 *The Rag and Bone Shop:* Truths That Shape the Soul 52

5 *Frenchtown Summer:* Reflections of Other Cormier Works 68

Chronology of Robert Cormier's Major Works 78

Selected Teacher Resources 79

Works Cited 83

ACKNOWLEDGMENTS

Authentic classroom discussion and student writing are essential in a book such as this, and I am grateful to have worked with three extraordinary English teachers who use Robert Cormier's works in their classes and agreed to share their results with me. Melanie Loew of Howland High School in Warren, Ohio, has successfully taught *After the First Death* to her advanced ninth graders for several years, and Traci O'Brian of Glenwood Middle School in Youngstown, Ohio, has used *Tunes for Bears to Dance To* with her seventh graders several times. She agreed also to try *The Rag and Bone Shop* for the first time and was pleased with her students' responses. Similarly, Colleen Ruggieri of Boardman High School in Youngstown, Ohio, had never taught *Heroes* to her eleventh graders but was excited to include it in her curriculum. I am grateful, also, to the principals of these schools—Frank Thomas, Anthony Alvino, and Timothy Saxton, respectively—whom I commend for agreeing to allow the students and teachers to participate in this project.

I am also indebted to the Youngstown State University Research Council for its financial support and to Heinemann Executive Editor Lisa Luedeke, whose interest in this project and in the Young Adult Literature Series encouraged my efforts.

Finally, I thank my husband, Paul, and my daughters, Jennifer and Michele, whose continuing question "How's the book coming?" kept me on task when I was easily distracted by retirement and relocation.

Discovering Robert Cormier

One of my most frightening teaching assignments came when I was student teaching at an urban high school years ago. When I learned that *A Tale of Two Cities* was part of the required curriculum for tenth grade, and that I would have one section of "general" tenth graders, I scrambled to find ways to teach them this difficult novel. Some, I know, never read the book, and many of those who tried were lost in Dickens' long descriptions and multiple plot strands. It was a painful experience for all of us. Though I loved reading Dickens, my students didn't share my enthusiasm, and I was too inexperienced to know how to engage them. I wish I had known then about Robert Cormier's work.

It wasn't until I was teaching ninth-grade English in the late 1970s that I first became acquainted with Robert Cormier's books. Our school librarian happened to attend a meeting at which he was the featured speaker, and she brought me copies of *I Am the Cheese* and *The Chocolate War*. I'm forever indebted to that wonderful lady because she introduced me to the works of perhaps the greatest author of young adult books that our profession has seen. I must admit, though, that I was reluctant at the time to share Cormier's books with my ninth graders because of their seemingly depressing content, so I tried them out on my eleventh graders in an independent reading class. My students were fascinated by his novels, and I overheard many a hallway discussion about what exactly happened to Adam Farmer in *I Am the Cheese*. And both males and females were riveted by *The Chocolate War*, telling me how much they could relate to Jerry Renault's plight in battling peer pressure. Word got around, and soon other students were knocking on my door, asking to borrow the books.

Later, when I became a faculty member in the English Department at Youngstown State University, I was a member of the committee that invited Cormier to be guest author at our annual English Festival, attended by over 3,000 students, teachers, and librarians each year. He came to help us celebrate our tenth anniversary, and I volunteered to be his escort to and from campus. What a wonderful opportunity to have extended conversations about his books and to learn more about this exceptional author. Five years later, he came back again to participate in the Festival's fifteenth anniversary celebration as one of our most popular authors. Though some adults were disturbed by what they viewed as the darkness in his books, they were impressed by his unassuming, grandfatherly manner and listened intently to everything he had to say. The students welcomed him enthusiastically, giving him a standing ovation each time he took the stage.

As I came to know Bob Cormier over the years, I realized more and more just what a special person he was—so humble about his work and so grateful that teachers were making his books available to students. One of my fondest memories concerns a call I made to him on New Year's Eve one year. A colleague and I were working on a conference proposal that focused on some of Bob's books, when we had the bright idea to invite him to be a panelist. When I boldly dialed his number and he answered the phone, I could barely speak. When he said he would love to do it, I was at a loss for words. Needless to say, he packed the house at our NCTE session in Pittsburgh the following November.

When Bob passed away on November 2, 2000, the world of young adult literature went into mourning. We would have no more of his extraordinary books, no more of his presentations, no more conversations with the man who cared so passionately about young people and the world they live in. Our only consolation is that he comes alive for us again every time we read one of his works, and his books have received renewed attention and criticism. Always the target of censorship, his novels have weathered many storms over the years in school districts around the country, and he made numerous appearances in support of teachers who were being challenged for teaching his works.

During the summer of 2002, I taught a graduate course that I titled "A Little Touch of Cormier in the Night," my whimsical parody of the phrase, "A little touch of Harry in the night," spoken by Henry when he tries to rally his troops to battle in Shakespeare's *Henry V*. The comparison is apt, I think, because, like Henry, Cormier attempts in his books to rally his young adult readers to awareness of the dangers inherent in institutional corruption, societal greed, and familial deception. And in spite of the criticism that his books are too disturbing for young people, close study of his work reveals that his novels do provide hope, though sometimes unconventionally and not always happily.

While the students in my class, many of whom were secondary school English teachers, appreciated Bob's writing and wanted to share it with their students, they feared censorship attempts by community and school individuals. They were uncertain about how they might bring his books into the curriculum and how they might approach teaching his works. As they were writing their papers and designing their projects, some of them asked me for help in rationalizing to parents and administrators the teaching of Cormier's works. Others wanted help with approaches and ideas for studying his novels with students. It was my work with this class, along with my own experience teaching Bob's works over the years, that caused me to see the need for a book that could help all English teachers bring his works into their classrooms.

I have chosen to focus in this book on some of Bob's more recent works because there have been quite a few articles written about teaching his earlier books such as *The Chocolate War* and *I Am the Cheese*, and many teachers are already using these books in their classrooms. The only exception to this decision is my inclusion of *After the First Death*, first published in 1979 by Pantheon. Because this book is more timely than ever today, I see it as a valuable component of this volume.

Teaching the Selected Works of Robert Cormier, like all the books in this Heinemann subseries, is not meant to be a critical assessment of the author's work. Neither is it biographical, as Patty Campbell's *Presenting Robert Cormier*, Updated Edition, and her latest book, *Robert Cormier: Daring to Disturb the Universe*, serve both purposes well and, indeed, work well as companions to this text. Rather, the purpose of this book is to help teachers find ways to bring Bob's works to their students with courage and conviction, confident that the novels will be a valuable addition to their curriculum and that their students will benefit intellectually, socially, and emotionally from reading them.

After the First Death
Dealing with the World as It Is

Robert Cormier quotes the last line of Dylan Thomas' poem "A Refusal to Mourn the Death, by Fire, of a Child in London" as the inscription for his novel *After the First Death*. It's not hard to understand why. Like most of his novels, the book is about the loss of innocence and the exploitation of the young by corrupt or misguided adults. Young people die in this book, a fact that many readers find hard to take. But the book is about so much more: blind patriotism, betrayal, the relationship between father and son, the confusion and longings of adolescence, the frightening power of institutions.

Perhaps most disturbing of all, this novel may be more relevant today than when it was published in 1979. Terrorism continues to threaten the lives and freedoms of people around the world, and the young are not immune. Though the terrorists' methods in this novel may seem rather tame compared with today's bombings and beheadings, the young protagonists in *After the First Death* struggle with the same doubts, fears, and uncertainties as the young adult readers who find the book so compelling. Kate wonders if she is brave enough to fend off the terrorists and save the children entrusted to her care. Ben craves the love and respect of his father, only to be betrayed as a result of his trust. And Miro, trained to be a terrorist from his boyhood days, is torn between his natural youthful inclinations and the horrific demands of loyalty to his homeland.

Cormier has said that he set out to write a love story when he began *After the First Death*. Even though it didn't turn out that way, young adult readers seem to sense the possibilities in the relationship between Miro and Kate. He is fascinated by her, and she can't resist flirting with him, even though she finds him repulsive. The complexity of Cormier's characters in this book is not lost on adolescent readers, nor are the intricacies of his plot and style. Students may either love or hate the book, but either way they are fully engaged and capable of demonstrating deep insight, if given the chance to examine their reactions in a classroom setting.

We may read and study *After the First Death* through several different perspectives: literary, sociological, psychological, and/or political. Each approach can illuminate the novel in some way, while encouraging students to make connections between the fictional events of the book and the real world.

The Literary Perspective

Response Journals

When she assigns *After the First Death* to her ninth-grade honors English class, Melanie Loew asks the students to keep a response journal in which they can ask questions, make observations, and generally comment on the book as they are reading. The reader response strategy of beginning with the students' curiosity about a work opens the door to the kind of literary exploration English teachers relish. About an early chapter introducing Ben, one student writes, "He said he doesn't need a psychiatrist, but he is talking about committing suicide. Did he attempt suicide before? Where were his parents? Does he live alone? He doesn't feel a connection with his father." Later, reading about Miro, she asks, "Is Miro related to Artkin? It's hard to believe his conscience can handle these deaths he will cause. He reminds me of Ben a little." And when

Miro meets Kate, she observes, "I think Miro feels sorry for the girl. All his talk was unhappy, but then he talks about love." And she speculates, "He and Kate are becoming more personal. This will probably make it harder to kill her." At another point she wonders about the General's motivation in sending Ben as a decoy to the terrorists. "Why did he suggest his own son?" she asks. "I feel nervous for Ben," she adds. Again, she wonders, "Was Artkin really [Miro's] father? Why wouldn't he have told him, though?" And as she begins to understand the final chapter, she first asks, "Did Ben live?" Then, reading further, she observes, "The father can't bring himself to cope with this and admit things." She questions Ben's words to his father, "You killed me twice." Then she adds, "Oh, I get it now."

Asking these many questions obviously helped this student better understand the characters and the thrust of the plot, not an easy task since Cormier switches point of view with each chapter. Another student was annoyed by this voice shift, commenting, "I don't like the way the author writes. It's confusing how the point of view changes in every part." And he didn't like Cormier's emphasis on Kate's urinary problems, commenting, "Why does the author use so much detail describing Kate wetting her pants? It seems unnecessary." This student approached the response journal a little differently, making frequent observations and analyzing the characters and their motivations. Considering Ben, he observes, "Ben is the writer in first person. . . . The *Bridge* is important. Also, he's been shot. He's random, and he contradicts himself. Obviously father-son issues. He betrayed someone/something. Took sleeping pills." Then he begins to analyze. "Miro and Ben are similar; both feel out of place. Might have identity issues. They're about the same age." Of Artkin he says, "Artkin likes acting, adapting, and messing with people. Can be compared to a chameleon. You drop your guard when you see it." By the end of the story, this student still isn't sure what happened, as he writes, "I didn't quite understand this part. Is Ben dead? Did he jump off the bridge?" Now he begins asking questions: "Miro is alone now and has to act independently. Will he continue to fight for his cause, or will he just abandon it?"

Beginning the study of this novel with response journals emphasizes student engagement with the text as the first step to deeper understanding. Students become more aware of their subjective responses to the characters and events, perhaps paving the way for more objective analysis later on. The next step might be to form small groups where each student can present his or her questions for discussion. For example, the first student quoted is curious about the relationship between Miro and Kate. Perhaps this can be explored in more detail by members of the group. In what sections of the novel do we see Kate and Miro together? How does their relationship progress from early in the hijacking to the final chapters? Was Kate merely toying with Miro to keep herself and the children alive, or was she really attracted to him? What evidence do we see of that? Did Miro have romantic feelings for Kate, or was it merely lust, since he hadn't ever been with a girl before? Why does he end up killing her in the end?

The second student seems concerned about Miro's and Ben's identity issues. Do other students in the group have similar concerns? How can we tell that these two are confused about their identity? What do they do and say that causes us to suspect this? In what ways are they similar? In what ways are they different? How much does their upbringing have to do with their confusion?

Tapping the students' questions about the characters in *After the First Death* could be a natural lead-in to a lesson on character development. Instead of beginning by asking abstractly, How do we come to understand fictional characters? (by what they say, what they do, and what other characters say about them), we use the students' curiosity as our starting point, making the lesson more meaningful and specific.

Group Poetry Unit

To further enrich the students' study of *After the First Death*, Melanie follows this response journal activity with a group poetry unit based on the novel and focused on figurative language. After assigning the students to groups of four, she has every group consider the following twelve categories:

- colors and/or rocks
- shapes and/or geographic formations
- music: song titles, lyrics, instruments, musicians

- animal kingdom
- literary genres
- beverages
- toys and/or tools
- entrees and/or desserts
- household appliances
- punctuation marks and/or traffic signs
- fruits and/or vegetables
- plants

The groups must then come up with something—a word, a phrase, an image—related to each category to create a poem about a character from *After the First Death*, italicizing any quoted lines from the novel. Jen, Kathy, Tara, and Scott wrote this poem, "Disguise of Innocence," about Miro:

> You're poison ivy, innocent to the naked eye, but poisonous to the touch.
>> A broken mirror displaying images of a distorted mind.
> From the beginning you've been an onion grown to make people cry.
> Your changing personality is like a chameleon constantly changing colors to disguise its true self.
>> A volcanic anger waiting to erupt.
> Hidden among mountains you want to stand out, and wait till your time finally comes.
>> Your life is a mystery, and I wish I could flip right to the end.
>> I'm predicting you can't hold a fairy tale ending.
>> A deadly sweet devil's food cake which every lie has eaten up.
>> You're a Bloody Mary, the tomato taste with an alcohol sting,
> Burning in my chest like the deadly bullet that tore through Kate.
> Disguised behind a rock hard exterior, hiding the truth of a metamorphic child who changes under pressure.
>> A bridge displaying a sign reading "slippery when wet," you make people
>>> want to lose control and slide over the edge.

"Your wounds of childhood just won't heal, the pain you feel is just too
real"*

With Artkin being the puppeteer, he controls your behavior with short
strings.

They were like puppets here on the bridge, and Sedeete held the strings.

*A line from "My Immortal" by Evanescence

Mounting their poem on bright yellow construction paper adorned
with graphics of a slice of devil's food cake, an onion, and a "Slippery
When Wet" sign, this group obviously had a strong sense of Miro's character and the turmoil he experiences throughout the novel. They saw the
"innocent monster" that Cormier so masterfully created.

Another group chose to write about Ben. Their poem is titled
"Buried Tragedy":

Shattered shale whispers a story of the dove with broken wings.
Sorrowful melancholy rising out of the wooden flute,
A lonely melody echoing the tragedy of a child named Ben.
Ashen rock lies by his sunken spirit,
Engulfed in this foamy sea of green
As every ounce of liquid is his tear of remorse.

He was so predictable.
Outlining the animal his spirit personified,
You always know what those creatures will do next.
Ben was foolish enough to take the whiskey of guilt and shame.
Too much of it can leave you drunk.
Dear child.

He might have been older. A man.
Yet inside he was not ready.
Ben should have gone back to those games
And molded more colorful pieces of clay.
Here is a piece of blue.
Small. Round. Insignificant.

Those blueberries he picked at Grandma's house
She rewarded him with her chocolate cupcakes dripping with vanilla
  icing
They would rise in the oven saturated with hope,
On a mission to perhaps become something great,
Only to be devoured.
Everything in life can symbolize Ben if you think about it hard enough.

Anyway,
Ben lived a life
Until something exploded,
Seeing that *cluster of firecrackers going off like miniature machine guns,*
Like tin foil in a microwave.
He just didn't belong.

Maybe Ben should have seen a stop sign before . . .
Cancel whatever had to be done.
It is too late now.
The End has arrived.

These students create a lonely, somber mood with their poem, capturing Ben's sadness and *naivete*, as they use sensory imagery to describe his "sunken spirit."

Melanie follows this writing activity with an evaluative exercise, giving each group a form to complete that invites them to look at their poem more critically and requires them to document the contribution of each group member (see Figure 1–1).

Student-Designed Discussion Questions

In her teaching guide for *After the First Death*, written for Perma-Bound's Living Literature Series, Mary Ellen Snodgrass includes a section she calls "Meaning Study," where she provides quotes from the novel, along with page numbers, and asks students to explain the meaning of each. A response approach to this activity might instead ask readers to jot down what *they* think are significant passages as they read and later to share these passages in pairs or groups, discussing their meaning and importance. An alternate activity would be to ask students to choose one pas-

AFD **Handout**
Evaluate Your Poem

Title of Your Group's Poem _____

List the poets in your group. After each name indicate the poet's contribution to the poem.

1.

2.

3.

4.

Indicate the line number of your poem in which your group feels it has dealt with the categories below. (You do not have to address the categories in the order they are listed.)

Explain why or how you feel this line, phrase, or word meets the categorical requirement.

1. Colors and/or rocks _____

2. Shapes and/or geographic formations _____

3. Music: song titles, lyrics, instruments, musicians _____

4. Animal kingdom _____

5. Literary genres _____

6. Beverages _____

7. Toys and/or tools _____

8. Entrees and/or desserts _____

9. Household appliances _____

10. Punctuation marks and/or traffic signs _____

11. Fruits and/or vegetables _____

12. Plants _____

FIGURE 1–1 *AFD Poem Evaluation*

sage they selected and explain in writing why they feel it's important to the story. Both activities require students to pay close attention to the novel as they read and to think more deeply about characters, plot events, and their reactions to the author's style and tone.

In discussing and writing about a work of literature, students sometimes have trouble moving from the literal level of comprehension to the more abstract interpretive and analytical levels. Rather than ask teacher-formulated questions at each of these levels, we might invite them to create their own questions, after discussing with them the various levels of cognitive responses based on Benjamin Bloom's Taxonomy of Educational Objectives, as described by Cline and McBride (1983) in *A Guide to Literature for Young Adults*:

Knowledge. Questions are based on specific facts, recall, and knowing what happened. Who are the characters? What did they do? When and where did they do it?

Interpretation. Questions examine the motives of the characters. What reasons do they have for acting and reacting as they do? What might be the consequences of their actions?

Application. Questions apply the characters' experiences to the readers' lives. For example, how would students react if Miro moved into their town? How well would Ben Marchand be accepted in their school? This level invites role-playing, as well as discussion.

Analysis. "Questions examine the structure of the plot, the use of symbolism, the development of characters, the resolution of conflicts, the style of the author, and the use of literary devices" (1983, 100). This is the level at which students move from subjective response to objectivity. Cline and McBride caution, however, that teachers should be keenly aware of their students' level of understanding. While the learning of mature readers may be enhanced by this kind of study, inexperienced or reluctant readers may not be ready to explore the work in such detail and may lose interest.

Synthesis. These questions tap students' ability to "arrange familiar elements into a new pattern" (101). This could mean placing characters in a different setting or taking characters from *After the First Death* and several other books and putting them into conversation with each other.

Evaluation. Questions may include both internal and external judgments. "If the evaluation is *internal*, the students will be looking at the elements within the novel to see if the best effects were achieved" (101). Was the ending logical? Were any events contrived by the author to achieve a specific effect? *External* evaluation can include comparing this novel with others Cormier has written, or comparing it with another novel by a different author written on a similar theme or with other selections written in the same time period.

After discussing Bloom's taxonomy with the class, we might divide the class into six groups and assign a category to each group, inviting them to come up with three or four questions/activities that fit their particular category. One representative from each group may write their questions on the board for class discussion, or, if time allows, students may put their questions on a transparency for viewing the following class period. Following are examples of possible questions/activities:

Knowledge. Who are the three protagonists in the novel? (As simple as this question may seem, it does test whether the students have read the book and their knowledge of the term *protagonist.*)

Interpretation. Why is Miro determined that Kate will be his "first death"?

Application. In what way do the adults in this novel resemble people you know? How and why?

Analysis. What is the effect on the reader of Cormier using alternating points of view in this novel?

Synthesis. What if Miro and Ben had been given the chance to talk to each other? Create a possible conversation between them. Role-play your conversation with someone in the class and explain why these two characters spoke as they did.

Evaluation. Was it necessary to the story for Miro to kill Kate? Why or why not?

The Sociological Perspective

Gender Roles

In addition to studying the literary aspects of the novel, reading *After the First Death* also affords us the opportunity to examine our assumptions about male-female behavior, the motivation for that behavior, and the consequences that follow. Students usually respond well to the following activities, but teachers must take care not to pit one gender against another.

1. As a prereading exercise ask small groups of students (mixed males and females) to make a list of what they consider to be typical male behaviors and typical female behaviors. After reading *After the First Death*, revisit their lists and discuss how much these assumptions influenced the way they read the novel.

2. Ask small groups of students to write a list of questions they wish to direct to a character in *After the First Death*. Then ask them to examine their lists and determine how many questions were written to male characters and how many to females. What kinds of questions were directed to each? Why? Use the results as the basis for a discussion of gender roles as they connect to both the novel and the students' lives.

3. Divide the class into male-female pairs by lottery (matching numbers picked at random). With the male students assuming the persona of a female character from the novel and vice versa, have each pair create

and rehearse a short dialogue that illuminates some particular conflict in the story. Ask each pair to role-play their dialogue for the class. Discuss the experience of becoming a person of the opposite gender. What problems did they encounter? How did they resolve these problems? In what way did the experience help them understand the character better—or if it didn't help, why not?

Cultural Differences

The whole idea of a young person being so attached to a scarcely remembered homeland that he would kill to win it back is foreign to most American adolescents. In the case of Miro Shantas, all he remembers is Artkin rescuing him and his brother Aniel and educating them in the ways of terrorism. When Aniel is killed, Miro is haunted by the memories of his brother. He is adamant about killing the bus driver because the man's death would be a test of his manhood, marking his long-awaited entry into the terrorist brotherhood. Yet when Miro sees that the driver is actually a young woman, Kate Forrester, his response is a mixture of disgust that she is not what he expected and attraction to her blonde good looks. In spite of his resistance to this attraction, Miro frequently steals glances at Kate as she tries to console the children on the bus during the course of their capture. He has never seen an American girl up close before, and he both loves and hates what he sees. His culture demands that he have nothing to do with the likes of Kate, yet his innate adolescent curiosity causes him to struggle throughout the novel. We learn that he has listened to and likes Elvis Presley's music, something Kate finds mildly amusing, given the circumstances of the hijacking.

And Kate—a carefree young woman who never had to worry about anything more serious than whether she would win the lead in the school play—what does she make of this dark, mysterious young man who may hold her life in his hands? True to her experience, she resorts to the only way she knows to distract him: flirting. Though she is repulsed by him in many ways, Kate can't resist leading him on by talking to him about his homeland and his past, trying to gain his trust. She knows nothing about his background or the cultural forces that have molded him for seventeen years into an unfeeling, almost robotic person. As

Patty Campbell (1989) points out in *Presenting Robert Cormier*, this is where Kate learns that "innocence" can be evil as well as good, when Miro "looked at her with innocent eyes as he told her of killing people" (Campbell 1989, 108). Kate is innocent, too—innocent of realizing that her taunting of Miro at the end of the story would prove fatal. Not understanding how deep his cultural roots were, or how significantly they determined his actions, she underestimates him, resulting in her death.

Students reading this novel have an excellent opportunity to write about and discuss the ways in which cultural differences influence our behavior. Because of the current conflict in the Middle East, it may be more important than ever to help students understand the social, economic, and religious forces that shape Middle Eastern culture. If possible, it would be best to avoid politics when using this cultural approach, as students' thinking could be negatively influenced before they even start their exploration.

1. Before reading the novel, ask students to write a journal response to this question: What do you know about the culture of the Middle East? Put the entry aside, then assign groups of students to research various countries of the Middle East and aspects of their culture: food, religious customs, dress, architecture, economics, music, art, and so on. Groups may then present their findings to the class in creative ways, ultimately discussing the similarities and differences they see between Middle Eastern culture and American culture. Have students revisit their journal entries and write a new entry explaining what they know now that they didn't know previously about the Middle East.

2. Invite an expert on Middle Eastern culture to speak to the class. Encourage students to ask questions about their curiosities and concerns.

3. Ask a student to take on the persona of Miro being interviewed by the class. Have the rest of the class come prepared with questions they would like to ask Miro about his culture and how it influenced his behavior throughout the novel.

4. An alternative to the previous option might be for the students to write a letter to Miro, asking him the same questions, then to exchange letters with another student and have that student take on Miro's persona in replying to the letter.

Psychological Perspective

Identity Development

In her *ALAN Review* article, "The Psychological Changes of Adolescence: A Test of Character," Sharon Stringer (1994) writes about identity development as demonstrated in young adult literature. She explains specifically five key concepts on which research in identity development is based:

- *Moratorium (experimentation with roles)*. As defined by psychologists Erik Erikson and James Marcia, this is a period of experimentation that is essential for the individual to attain identity.

- *Fidelity (making an informed commitment)*. As defined by Erikson, the adolescent, after experimenting with different roles and value systems, makes an ideological commitment, discovers someone to believe in, or finds a cause to be true to without blindly obeying others.

- *Emotional Autonomy (gaining a sense of self)*. According to psychologist Lawrence Steinberg, one component in the development of emotional autonomy is the deidealization of parents. Psychologist Eastwood Atwater notes that the individual handles criticism, hurdles, and setbacks constructively at this stage by developing inner strength and self-esteem.

- *Identity Confusion (impediment to identity achievement)*. As defined by both Erikson and Marcia, the individual has not made a firm commitment to any particular vocation or ideology. This may lead to adolescents' isolation, chronic delinquency, or suicide.

- *Identity Foreclosure (impediment to identity achievement)*. Individuals choose an identity that parents or peers select for them, without taking time to experiment with different roles and never questioning their beliefs. (29)

Although these concepts are abstract and may be difficult for students to grasp, when we connect them to the behavior of fictional characters that students care about, they suddenly become meaningful. Take Kate, for example. Having played the role of the "all-American girl" all her life, she is thrust into a situation that challenges her perception of self. After reviewing the previous concepts, we might ask students to write about or discuss the following questions:

- What psychological changes does Kate undergo as she copes with the responsibility of a busload of small children and the reality of death at the hands of terrorists?

- How does Kate feel about herself when we first meet her in the novel? How does her thinking and behavior change as the novel progresses? How does she feel about herself at the end? What does this say about her psychological growth?

Then we can turn to Miro. Cormier has written and spoken about his "monstrous innocence," born of the life he has led, a young man trained by terrorists to kill or be killed. We might ask:

- Which of the aspects of identity development do you see in Miro? In what way(s) are they apparent?

- Does Miro elicit pity or hatred from you as a reader? Why?

- Based on what you've learned about Miro from the story, what do you expect he will do now that he is alone and on his own? Why?

As we study Kate and Miro, we must also study Ben. Though he seems to be a more shadowy character in the story than Kate and Miro, since we are never sure whether it is he speaking or his schizophrenic father, Ben does elicit a strong response from us as readers. Students might explore these questions:

- What connection do you see between Ben and Miro in this novel?

- Which aspects of identity development do you see in Ben? In what way(s) are they apparent?

- Based on his actions, do you admire Ben or feel sorry for him? Why?

- Is Ben alive or dead at the end of the novel? How do you know?

Further Activities to Explore Identity Development

1. *Moratorium.* Brainstorm as a class the different roles adolescents play. Ask students to reflect in their journals on the roles they've played in their lives. Whom did they try to be? Why? What was the result? Then examine the roles played by Kate, Miro, and Ben. (This examination could perhaps lead to an essay on the value to identity achievement of role experimentation.)

2. *Fidelity.* Ask students to write a journal entry reflecting on different roles they've experimented with (e.g., macho guy, sophisticated girl, fashion leader, class clown, star student). Then ask them to reflect on people whose value systems they've admired (e.g., parents, teachers, film stars, music artists, peers). Discuss as a class how and when this experimentation and admiration occurred and whether and how they came to settle on a specific role and set of values in their lives—or if they are still experimenting. This might lead to more research, culminating in an analytical paper on the relationship among experimentation, fidelity, and identity achievement.

3. *Emotional Autonomy.* Have students in small groups discuss the influence of parents and peers on their lives (or they might cite instances in their journals). Ask students to write a letter thanking someone who has been influential in their lives in some way. Survey the class to determine whether the letters were written to parents, peers, or others. Discuss the influence of parents, peers, and other adults on the characters in *After the First Death* and how that influence promotes or impedes emotional autonomy.

4. *Identity Confusion.* Talk about the importance of belonging to a group. Brainstorm what might happen when an adolescent feels isolated or left out. Have small groups discuss how identity confusion affects the characters in the novel.

5. *Identity Foreclosure.* Explore in journals how children follow in parents' footsteps or try to be like peers in choice of dress, career, politics, and/or religion. Discuss whether this is good or bad and how it might interfere with identity achievement. Explore the issue further in discussion of Kate, Miro, and Ben. (Students might also create and perform skits showing what happens when adolescents conform and don't conform.)

Father-Son Relationships

For adolescents, relationships with their peers, especially those of the opposite gender, are usually primary. Equally important, however, are their relationships with parents. Cormier focuses especially on father-son relationships in *After the First Death*—namely, Ben's relationship with the General and Miro's relationship with Artkin. Though it's never confirmed in the novel that Artkin is Miro's father, all the signs are there—especially the manner of Kate's death when she confronts Miro with this realization at the end of the novel. Cormier himself has admitted to the connection, and this plot device creates tension throughout the book.

Though students will identify more closely with the three young protagonists in this novel, they may also find it interesting to examine the thinking and behavior of the two "fathers" in the story, General Marchand and Artkin. Ben closely identifies with his father, the General. Indeed, Cormier builds part of the novel on the confusion of the Ben/General personality. Like Artkin, the General is a patriot who sacrifices his son to The Cause. Unlike Artkin, the General lives to regret it. On the one hand, the father dies, leaving the son to terrorize again; on the other, the son dies, leaving the father schizophrenic and unable to function. Students might think about these questions:

- What is the relationship between Ben and the General? How do we learn of their relationship in the novel?

- What is the relationship between Miro and Artkin? What events from the novel demonstrate their relationship?

- How are Ben's and Miro's actions influenced by their relationships with their fathers?

- Is Miro truly Artkin's son? What events from the story support your answer?

- What happens to General Marchand at the end of the novel? How do you know?

Political Perspective

Cormier was ahead of his time when he published *After the First Death* in 1979. Though airplane hijackings were in the news at that time, the author could scarcely imagine what lay ahead in 2001 and thereafter when it came to terrorism. It's ironic (and perhaps a blessing for him) that he passed away ten months before the horrific events of September 11, 2001. Few would disagree that most of Cormier's novels are political, but he was careful about specificity in this novel, refraining from naming the homeland referred to by Artkin and Miro and giving the terrorists generic names that only hinted at Middle Eastern origin. As Patty Campbell (1989) tells us, "Cormier has no intention of taking sides in any actual political controversy; he has more important and more eternal matters to consider" (104). Yet, he does examine the politics of the institution—in this case, the military—as he explores how far a father would go in endangering his son in the name of patriotism.

Given the state of the world today, it's impossible not to associate the terrorists in *After the First Death* with certain Middle Eastern countries, and it would be virtually impossible to avoid discussing student concerns at some point, preferably after they have a chance to examine the culture of the Middle East. Perhaps the hardest thing for students to do is to see terrorists as people. In the eyes of the world they are monsters, and Cormier explores this idea chillingly in his characterization of Miro. April D. Nauman (1999) examines the ways in which fictional characters can influence how children learn about real people. She says:

> In the good guy/bad guy schema, we . . . are never on the bad-guy side. Therefore the other guy—the "not we," the one who is different—must be. The notion that there are easily identifiable bad guys and good guys is part of what enables humans to commit acts of violence against others, which is why it is useful in the socialization of future soldiers. (115)

Though Nauman is talking here about the Nazis as they are portrayed in Lois Lowry's *Number the Stars*, her insights can be applied to the terrorists, as well:

> these easy-to-hate flat characters contain no clue that the Germans at that point in history were ever anything but evil, and the question of how a nation of people *becomes* fascist never arises . . . the more difficult question [is] how the German people could have come to commit such monstrous acts. (117)

If our students have previously studied the history and culture of the Middle East, they may better understand how terrorist extremists became so violent and why they continue to be so. Miro and his older brother Aniel were just little boys when Artkin began training them to hate and kill. As abhorrent as this may be to us, it underscores the fact that terrorists are made, not born. We might begin by asking students the following questions:

- Are Miro and Artkin "flat characters"? Do they grow and change, or do they remain the same throughout the novel? On what do you base your answer?

- Cormier makes the point that Miro was good at languages in school. What other kinds of things do you suppose he was learning? What events in the novel support your view?

- Is Miro's allegiance to Artkin based on love, respect, or fear? How do you know?

Censorship

As with all of Cormier's novels, censorship attempts have forced teachers to defend the use of *After the First Death* in the classroom. Complaints have ranged from dismay at the frequent references to Kate's bladder problem, to shock at the terrorists' drugging of little children, to horror at the wanton killing of young Raymond by the terrorists. While these last two events are certainly horrific, they are indicative of terrorist behavior, demonstrating just how far such desperate people will go to promote their cause. These people are not role models for the young. In fact, Cormier was quick to defend his books against charges of poor or absent role models and dark, depressing plots. In a 1985 interview with Anita Silvey, quoted by Kathy Neal Headley, Cormier stated, "I can't be concerned with that. I'm not worrying about corrupting youth. I'm worrying about writing realistically and truthfully to affect the reader. What I worry about is good taste and getting my message across by whatever means I can" (Headley 1994, 2). And that message is a weighty one, as underscored by author Lois Duncan, who reminds us in her article, "Breaking the Rules," that none of Cormier's characters is concerned with "alcoholism, drug use (except where imposed by institutions), premarital sex, childbirth, physical handicaps, social and racial problems, divorce, mental illness (except where imposed by institutions), and homosexuality" (1980, 1). No, Cormier has even more serious issues on his mind in his exploration of institutional politics and psychological intimidation, giving us and our students substantive grist for our intellectual mill.

In the classroom we can use the arguments criticizing *After the First Death* to promote critical thinking about censorship issues. Ideas include the following:

- Leading a class discussion about censorship in general and asking students what they know about censorship attempts in any aspect of life.

- Presenting small groups of students with specific censorship complaints about *After the First Death* and having them discuss the merits of the complaints.

- Asking students to research the censorship cases against Cormier's books and present their findings to the class.

- Creating a scenario of a censorship attempt to which students can respond in writing: *A parent of one of your classmates has complained to your school principal that your teacher is using* After the First Death *in your tenth-grade class. The parent demands that the book be withdrawn from the curriculum immediately and replaced with something more wholesome. Your teacher has asked your class to write a letter to the principal, telling her how you feel about this attempt to ban the book from your class.*

- Having pairs of students role-play the previous situation, with one person taking the role of the parent and another the role of the principal. A class discussion may follow.

Teacher Postscript

Though Melanie says she has never had a negative response to *After the First Death*, she and the curriculum director at her school decided to remove the book for the 2001 school year because of the events of 9/11. Of their reasons, she says, "We had no pressure from anyone; there was such pervasive unease that we felt the school bus scenario might be too much for already emotional ninth graders." Looking forward to subsequent years of teaching the novel, she adds:

> While I have worked with imagery and characterization in group-composed poetry in the past, I will probably explore the novel for social, psychological, and medical validity. Students will research topics from bladder control to stress to migraines; the protocol of hostage negotiations; youthful terrorists; and self-perception as an identity-determining factor. This gives me the opportunity to introduce credible secondary materials (print and/or electronic). My students have told me repeatedly that in spite of the 1979 copyright, they feel such relevance to certain parts of the plot. I may [continue] to do the poetry as well, since the ensuing discussion

leading to a collaborative decision of how to metaphorically characterize someone like Artkin as a household appliance or beverage provides some of the most engaging discussions all year.

Teacher Defenses

Because all good literature reflects life, English teachers should become familiar with writing rationales for works they teach, since any work can generate controversy. Two resources that will help are Louann Reid's *Rationales for Teaching Young Adult Literature* (Heinemann, 1999) and the CD *Rationales for Challenged Books* (NCTE/IRA, 1998). The latter contains a rationale for *After the First Death* ready for use. Another excellent resource on censorship in general is Pipkin and Lent's *At the Schoolhouse Gate: Lessons in Intellectual Freedom* (Heinemann, 2002). With the easy availability of these resources, no teacher need be caught unaware and defenseless against the censors. If we believe that what we are teaching is in our students' best interests, we owe it to them to stand up for our beliefs. As Melanie Loew's students have demonstrated, *After the First Death* is a book that merits our support; otherwise, why would we be teaching it in the first place?

Heroes
What Does It Mean to Be Heroic?

As we saw in the previous chapter on *After the First Death*, defining heroism can be difficult. Kate Forrester did not feel heroic, even though she gave her life trying to protect a busload of young children from terrorists. Ben Marchand did not even realize he might have been doing a heroic thing when he served as a messenger between the U.S. military and the terrorists. But, ironically, Miro Shantas assumed a heroic stance in his determination to kill and possibly give his life for his "cause" and for the homeland he did not even remember.

Robert Cormier is well aware of the ambiguity of the term *hero*, as he forces readers to examine once again the motivation and behavior of a young protagonist facing a life crisis in *Heroes* (1998). Eighteen-year-old Francis Cassavant returns from World War II horribly disfigured and determined to kill the man he idolized as a young teenager, a man who received the Silver Star for bravery in the same war. This man, Larry LaSalle, came to Monument, Francis' hometown, several years earlier and opened a recreation center, which the town affectionately dubbed the "Wreck Center," where the young people could socialize and dance. Charismatic and handsome, Larry easily won the hearts of the town's teenagers, including Francis. But there was a dark side to Larry, too, as Francis gradually began to realize. Uneasy about Larry's unusual interest in Nicole Renard, the girl whom Francis loved and hoped to win, Francis was stunned to witness what turned out to be Larry's rape of Nicole when Larry forced her to dance with him alone in the darkened Wreck Center one night. Francis, Larry, and Nicole had been the only people left at the Center after the celebratory party to welcome Larry home, and Larry had insisted that Francis leave so he could have one last dance with Nicole before the night ended. But something caused Francis to linger just outside the door, and what he overheard changed his life forever. Larry was forcing himself on Nicole. Shocked and guilt-ridden, Francis tried to apologize to Nicole for not rescuing her, but to no avail. He saw no alternative but to enlist, hoping to die in combat. Instead, his face was partially blown away when he intentionally fell on a grenade, leaving him disfigured and determined to kill Larry LaSalle. The irony of the situation is that Francis' fellow soldiers saw his falling on the grenade as an act of bravery rather than a suicide attempt, and he, like Larry, is also awarded the Silver Star.

Cormier cleverly forces us to examine the concept of *hero* throughout the novel. When Larry comes to town, his opening of the Wreck Center seems like an altruistic act. He wants to give the town's young people something constructive to occupy their time, "urging everyone to participate in at least one activity" (43). Since Francis is the narrator of the story, we see Larry only through his eyes. "Larry LaSalle was everywhere in the center," Francis tells us, taming the school bully by teaching him how to sing, guiding and encouraging a shy, gawky girl until she could dance "like a Broadway star" (44). Francis goes on:

> Rumors told us that Larry LaSalle had also been a star, performing in nightclubs in New York and Chicago. Someone brought in a faded newspaper clipping showing him in a tuxedo, standing beside a nightclub placard that read STARRING LARRY LASALLE. We knew little about him, however, and he discouraged questions. . . . Why did he turn his back on show business and return to Frenchtown? No one dared to ask him, although there were dark hints that he had "gotten into trouble" in New York City . . . (44–45)

Despite the rumors, Larry appeared to be above reproach, encouraging all the young people who came to the center to be "stars" in their own right, even taking Francis under his wing by teaching him to be a champion at table tennis. And he was certainly a war hero, saving an entire platoon and capturing an enemy machine gun nest, a heroic act to be sure.

But contradictions abound in this novel. Francis goes to war for selfish reasons, not to fight for his country. He fell on a grenade, hoping to be killed, but instead he received an award for bravery. If Larry's act was heroic, Francis' certainly was not. Instead, it is ironic. Yet Francis vowed to avenge Larry's attack on Nicole. Is attempted murder a heroic act if it's done to right a wrong?

When Francis confronts Larry in Larry's run-down apartment near the end of the novel, he finds a crippled, broken man. "No wounds that you can see," he tells Francis, "but I'm worn out. They called it jungle fever at first, but I don't think they really know what it is . . ." (112). A significant conversation takes place between the two at this point, which clearly addresses the good vs. evil theme at the heart of the novel:

> "You could have had anybody," I say, my voice too loud, booming in my ears. "All those beautiful ladies at the dance that night. Why Nicole?"
>
> "The sweet young things, Francis. Even their heat is sweet . . ."
>
> *Sweet young things.* Had he done it before? How many young girls had been invaded by him? I shake my head in dismay.
>
> "Everybody sins, Francis. The terrible thing is that we love our sins. We love the thing that makes us evil. I love the sweet young things."
>
> "That isn't love," I say.
>
> "There's all kinds of love, Francis."
>
> "Then, didn't you know that we loved you?" I say. "You were our hero, even before you went to war. You made us better than we were . . ."
>
> He sighs, his lips trembling, and his voice trembles, too, when he asks: "Does that one sin of mine wipe away all the good things?" (114–15)

And there lies the difficult question—significant substance for students to consider.

Prereading Activities

We can examine the idea of *hero* as we read and respond to this novel, by giving students a series of scenarios like those that follow, asking them to rank the actions from *most heroic* to *least heroic* and be prepared to explain their reasons:

- An accident leaves a gymnast paralyzed. For five years she spends twelve to fourteen hours a day in therapy trying to regain the use of her legs. Her hard work results in a miraculous recovery, and she wins a gold medal in the Olympics.

- A school teacher, invited to be part of the seven-person crew of the Space Shuttle, dies as the rocket explodes shortly after takeoff.

- An eleven-year-old boy who sees two men sexually assaulting a thirteen-year-old girl, threatening to kill her if she resists, rides off on his bicycle and informs the police. The officers arrive too late to prevent the rape, but the boy's actions may have saved the girl from being killed.

- A lifeguard rescues a six-year-old boy from drowning in a public pool by dragging him out with a hook.

- A scientist makes a discovery that will help cure thousands of people with heart disease.

As the students begin to compare and discuss their rankings in small groups, they have the opportunity to think more carefully about the concept of *hero*, preparing them to read the novel more critically as a result. The goal is not necessarily to reach a consensus on which action is most heroic, but to encourage thinking and discussion.

To begin her unit on *Heroes*, Colleen Ruggieri gives the students a handout listing quotes by famous people, attempting to define the term *hero* (see Figure 2–1). As a prereading activity, she asks the students to list individuals they consider to be heroes and their reasons why. She follows

What Is a Hero?

"How important it is for us to recognize and celebrate our heroes and she-roes!" —Maya Angelou

"My heroes are the ones who survived doing it wrong, who made mistakes, but recovered from them." —Bono

"Courage is more exhilarating than fear and in the long run it is easier. We do not have to become heroes overnight. Just a step at a time, meeting each thing that comes up, seeing it is not as dreadful as it appeared, discovering we have the strength to stare it down." —Eleanor Roosevelt

"If everybody was satisfied with himself, there would be no heroes." —Mark Twain

"Man's greatest actions are performed in minor struggles. Life, misfortunes, isolation, abandonment, and poverty are battlefields which have their heroes—obscure heroes who are at times greater than illustrious heroes." —Victor Hugo

"The history of the world is but the biography of heroes." —Thomas Carlyle

"The idol of today pushes the hero of yesterday out of our recollection; and will, in turn, be supplanted by his successor of tomorrow." —Washington Irving

"Often the test of courage is not to die but to live." —Vittorio Alfieri

"Success, or failure, very often arrives on wings that seem mysterious to us." —Dr. Marcus Bach

"Character is more important than intelligence for success." —Gilbert Beaux

"One's best success comes after their greatest disappointments." —Henry Ward Beecher

FIGURE 2–1

this three-minute activity with a class discussion, charting their choices and discussing their rationales.

About the results, she notes:

> "Soldiers" appeared and was discussed heavily; I think this had to do with September eleventh and its impact on the students' thinking. Other people who appeared on the class list were parents, grandparents, firemen, police officers, ambulance paramedics, and teachers. My class felt that celebrities and athletes are grossly overrated; however, they found it difficult to change public perception due to the intense media coverage of each individual.

Colleen follows this activity by asking students to create a list of five qualities that are universally present in all heroes, tying the results to the previous discussion. Next, she instructs them to bring in a photo of a heroic person, along with a description/biography, asking them to incorporate both on one sheet of paper for posting around the classroom. As a culmination to these prereading activities, students write a journal entry in response to at least one of the quotations on the original handout.

Multigenre Writing Assignments for *Heroes*

Letters

Colleen believes strongly in the multigenre approach to writing, and she presents a choice of several such assignments to her students. One of these assignments is a letter to a hero explaining why the student feels this person is heroic. One student wrote:

> Dear Lance Armstrong,
>
> Throughout the past few years of my life, you have always been a person that I admire and would consider a true American hero. Whenever I watch television, read the newspaper, or listen to the radio and hear your name, I always take a second to think how great a person you are and how you have inspired me, as well as probably millions of other people across the globe, to never give up and always keep fighting, no matter what. I do not

follow cycling very much, but when I heard that you were diagnosed with cancer I was still taken aback, for cancer is such a horrible disease that no person should ever have to experience during his/her lifetime.

For most athletes, I would assume that cancer is a career ending illness, so when you came back after your long fight with cancer I was in awe. I remember watching you win the Tour de France in 1999 and seeing my father's eyes well up with tears, for he was amazed by your unmatched determination, drive, and perseverance. Your tremendous comeback to cycling from your battle with cancer taught me that even when life seems to be heading in the wrong direction, I have to keep trying and never, ever give up. Seeing you still competing today reminds me to never let one event in my life ruin the years that I still have coming. You could have probably retired from cycling once you got rid of your cancer, just content to be alive. Lance, you are truly an inspiration and hero to me and I congratulate you on all of your accomplishments and wish you only the best in the years to come. God bless you!

Sincerely,
Rob Segreti

Rob clearly focuses on the concept of *hero* in his admiration for Lance Armstrong, successfully using the genre of letter writing to communicate his reasons. Assignments such as this encourage students to think more deeply through writing, helping them focus on the concept of *hero* as it relates to their personal lives and preparing them to make connections to the concept as it's presented by Cormier in the novel.

Poems for Two Voices
Still another writing assignment used by Colleen and her students is the poem for two voices, most notably popularized by Paul Fleischman in his Newbery Medal–winning book, *Joyful Noise* (Harper Trophy, 1988). Colleen asks the students to write their poems using the theme of forgiveness, hidden identity, or heroism. One student composed a poem she titled "Half and Half":

In the company of others I am me.	When alone I am me.
Dressed nicely,	Outfit a mess,

Hair in place,	Hair in a disheveled bun,
Make-up just right on my face.	My face washed and undone.
No thinking involved.	With thoughts my mind races
Teeth showing,	Tears running,
Lips smiling.	Lips frowning.
Costume on.	Costume off.
An actress in a show.	The person no one else knows.

Another student, taking on the persona of a soldier, wrote "The Voices of a War Hero":

Do it for your country	They all said so nonchalantly
I'll give my life for this	Which has brought nothing
honorable place	but pain
Destroy the enemy!	A human just like me
Show no mercy!	Just like the enemy has shown
They are the evil in	We are no better than they are . . .
this world	Where are the people who
	told me to come here?
	Where is my dad?
	Where is my help?
Fight for your country	I'm hurt
	I fought for my country . . .
Victory is *ours*	But now I just fight for my life
Together we will win	Alone—I will die

One of the strengths of this assignment is that it allows students to connect the novel in a very personal way to their fears or uncertainties, as the first student has done, or, more generally, to use this poetic genre to express their concerns about the society in which they live, as the second student chose to do. There is freedom within structure here, and students may even go further by composing such poems using the voices of characters from the same or other books they have read.

Interviews

Most students love to do interviews, and allowing the concept of *hero* to guide their choice of subject prompts thinking on their part and a sense of appreciation for the person they choose as hero. As another assignment choice, Colleen asks her students to interview someone they consider a hero, asking and recording the answers to at least fifteen questions. One student responded by interviewing her grandmother, whom she said she "adored." Portions of the interview follow:

Did you know much about Alzheimer's when you found out that Granddaddy had it?

No, not at all. But I learned quickly, and then I found out later that it ran in his family.

What was he like before the disease?

He was great. He was a strict father, but he loved each of his seven kids. He was a very fun grandfather, even if you can't remember him playing with you. He was always active. He worked very hard to make a life for his family.

What was the first sign Grandfather was becoming sick?

He forgot small things like dates and such. . . . I figured he had finally reached that age when things just began to slip from his memory. However, when he went to the doctor for his check-up, that's when we found out something was wrong.

How did you handle the news at first?

I was so lost. For a while, I didn't know what to do. There were lots of tears, but then I knew nothing was going to change—no matter how much I cried—this is how it was going to be. I had to deal with the situation.

Were there ever moments when you felt defeated?

Yes. I felt defeated all the time at first. Each day I'd get up hoping your grandfather would be better. But he still didn't know my name. He didn't know anyone. It just got worse. But then I realized this is how it is, and it's okay.

How did you overcome your sense of defeat?

With help from family, friends, and faith. Everyone around me was going through the same thing. It helped me to realize this. I prayed and prayed. Eventually I found peace. I also had a live-in nurse, who made things a lot easier.

Was there any humor in the disease?

Yes, actually there was. I thought it was funny to see all the grand-children run through the house, and even though he might not have known who you were, he still wanted to play with the kids. . . . Or he would try to scare you when you walked by and grab you by the arm and say, "BOO!" He thought that was a great game and so did all you kids.

What was the worst thing about his illness?

It was sad because it stole his identity. He got so bad that he had to wear a diaper. A grown man wearing a diaper just broke my heart. He couldn't remember anyone, even though he tried.

What was some of the "good" that came out of this misfortune?

It brought the family closer together. And it taught everyone a lesson about dealing with tragedy.

When Grandaddy passed away, what were your feelings?

I was ready for it. He hadn't been the person I had married for many, many years. He had suffered long enough. It was time.

Do you have any advice for someone who is suffering through the same ordeal?

I don't like to give advice because what worked for me might not work for everyone, but I'll tell you this: don't let anything overwhelm you. Somewhere somebody has it a lot worse. Just deal with the situation the best way you know how and remember that eventually you'll make it through.

Do you think this has made you stronger?

Of course I do. It didn't kill me—you know what they say: "If it does-n't kill you, it makes you stronger." I know I'm stronger because of it. Besides, I didn't do anything great; I just kept going.

This interview highlights a different kind of hero from those we so often see touted in the news media: a quiet hero whose everyday life is a testament to her strength and courage under stress. It's a heroic concept that deserves a place in classroom discussion—especially when talking about a novel like *Heroes*, where bravery (or cowardice) in war and justified or unjustified revenge are the issues.

Other Multigenre Assignments
Colleen offers her students other multigenre assignments based on *Heroes*, as well. One of these is to create a "Want Ad" for a hero. One student wrote:

Wanted: A Hero to Call My Own

Must be perfect in every way. No phoniness accepted. Must have overcome great difficulty and have worked immensely hard to get to where he or she is now. Good-looking celebrities only idolized for what is on the outside need not apply. I am looking for a hero living in the real world to mentor me, protect me, and love me for who I am now, and for the person that I will become with the aid and encouragement of my hero. I am in search of the ultimate superhuman to be my hero. If you exist, please call me at 000-000-0000. I won't be expecting your call.

Obviously the implication here is that real-life heroes are either hard to find or don't exist. Either way, this response to the assignment offers a good opportunity for discussion.

Colleen also gives her students the opportunity to create a CD of "hero songs" by famous artists. Students commonly choose Bette Midler's "Wind Beneath My Wings," Michael Bolton's "Go the Distance" from the movie *Hercules*, and "You Raise Me Up" by Josh Groban, among other songs. In addition to making the CD song list, students are asked to annotate each entry with an explanation of why they chose the song and how it relates to the concept of *hero*.

Since Cormier mentions the titles of several World War II songs in the novel, teachers may also want to make a CD of some of those songs to play for the class. "White Cliffs of Dover," "Don't Sit Under the Apple Tree," and, of course, "Dancing in the Dark" are most likely songs that students haven't heard before, and it's illuminating to listen to and discuss them after reading *Heroes*.

Group Discussion

Once students have read *Heroes*, getting them together in small discussion groups affords the opportunity to explore multiple questions about the novel. Colleen commonly asks each student to bring in four questions about the novel to share with the group, and she sometimes provides the following list of questions, as well:

- How does the novel make you question what a hero really is?

- How is the title of the book ironic?

- What is the significance of the quote, "Show me a hero and I will write you a tragedy," at the beginning of the novel?

- How would you analyze Larry LaSalle's character?

- How does this book make you think about the issue of appearance versus reality?

- What is the significance of the "Wreck Center" in terms of its name and its impact on the characters in the novel?

- Has this book changed the way you look at heroes? If so, how?

Using student-generated questions to begin small-group discussion makes that discussion even more meaningful because it stems from student curiosity about the novel. The teacher-generated questions may be used as a backup, either to further explore the story or to cover aspects of the novel not addressed in the students' questions. This response-centered approach to class discussion encourages student interpretation of *Heroes* and validates that interpretation significantly.

Heroes, published only two years before Cormier's death, is one of his last novels. Sadly, it has not received the publicity or acclaim of some of his earlier books and thus may not have found as much of a classroom audience. Still, teachers would do well to introduce the novel to their students for several reasons:

- It is based in a time rich in cultural history, as evidenced by the attitudes and actions of the characters in the novel.

- It examines a universal conflict—good vs. evil—that encourages substantive discussion.

- It affords the opportunity to make connections to other similarly themed literary works.

- It lends itself to a multigenre approach to teaching.

About teaching the novel, Colleen Ruggieri says:

My students truly enjoyed reading *Heroes* because it afforded them an opportunity to read a contemporary story that was not overwhelmingly difficult to comprehend. So often in American literature we read "the classics," and though my students appreciate the importance of such pieces, they often beg for reading material that is less "dry" or "difficult." I don't think that YA literature should ever fully replace the classics; however, I think that enriching the curriculum with such works really enhances student appreciation of the American experience. In most American literature courses, for example, students begin studies with Native American literature or Puritan writings—and the most modern works they read are *The Great Gatsby* or *Of Mice and Men*. I also enjoyed teaching *Heroes* because it was a quick unit that allowed me to assess students in creative ways.

Cormier usually begins each of his novels with an epigraph that reflects the content of the story. For *Heroes* he chose the quote from F. Scott Fitzgerald: "Show me a hero and I will write you a tragedy." Though *Heroes* is primarily about the tragedy of Francis Cassavant, we can't ignore the tragedy of Larry LaSalle, who, though he appears to be the antihero in the novel, suffers the tragedy of knowing what he could have been and realizing what he has become, wishing for death at Francis' hands. If these complex and thought-provoking themes of heroism and tragedy, so well presented by Cormier in this novel, are not worthy of classroom exploration, then much of what we call "classic literature" would lack worth as well. As Colleen points out in her earlier remarks, the study of American literature need not be limited to time-worn classics like *The Great Gatsby* and *Of Mice and Men*.

Tunes for Bears to Dance To
The Destruction of Innocence

Most of Robert Cormier's novels focus on older teenage protagonists; however, with *Tunes for Bears to Dance To* Cormier ventures into the world of eleven-year-old Henry Cassavant (no connection to Francis Cassavant of *Heroes*), a lonely boy trying to cope with moving to a new town after the unexpected death of his older brother, Eddie, and dealing with parents who seem too lost in their grief to notice him. Like many of Cormier's other works, *Tunes* explores the concept of *innocence*, this time in the person of Henry, who becomes caught in a Faustian web woven by his employer, Mr. Hairston, the grocer. Hairston's power over Henry highlights a second theme present in many of Cormier's novels—the abuse of power by adults over the young.

When Henry happens upon an old man, Mr. Levine, a Holocaust survivor, he becomes fascinated by the man's woodcarving talent and awed by the scope of the village the old man is carving as he re-creates his childhood home destroyed by the Nazis. But Mr. Hairston hates Mr. Levine, even though he's never met him, and Henry can't understand why. Henry's innocence, his grief at his brother's death, and his desire to please his parents and ease their suffering lead him to a moral struggle that no eleven-year-old should have to experience.

A common perception among teachers is that, while they might be willing to use Robert Cormier's works in their high school classes, they would be reluctant to teach them to middle school students. Several of the teachers in my graduate Cormier seminar expressed this fear, and censorship concerns were the primary reason. However, some teachers, like Traci O'Brian, have consistently included Cormier's works in their middle school curriculum. *Tunes for Bears to Dance To* is one novel that Traci uses successfully with her seventh-grade advanced students. She explains:

> I have been teaching *Tunes for Bears to Dance To* for five years. I had been interested in teaching a work by Robert Cormier at the middle school level because I thought students would enjoy his characters and their many internal conflicts. So many young adult novels involve physical conflicts and use violence to attract readers, so I wanted a change where students could identify with a character who may have had similar thoughts and feelings to those seventh graders might experience, including the feeling that they are living within the shadow of an older sibling and submitting to the pressure of authority figures.

Word Study

To be sure students understand the words they will encounter in the novel, Traci gives them a word study list as they begin reading, noting the page number on which the word can be found and asking them to list definitions using their own words rather than the dictionary. As a class, they define the words after every few chapters, examining the words in the context of the story. The second part of this assignment sheet deals with connotation, where Traci lists words like *crazy house* and *greaseball*, asking students to write a one- or two-word reaction for later discussion of how our word associations may ultimately influence our reading. (See Figure 3–1.)

Tunes for Bears to Dance To
Vocabulary/Word Study

Determine the meanings of the following vocabulary words. Be sure
to list definitions using your own words. Be prepared to use each
word correctly in a sentence on the test.

1. piazza (1): _____
2. tenement (3): _____
3. three-decker (3): _____
4. exploits (7): _____
5. fatigue (17): _____
6. bandannas (23): _____
7. monument (33): _____
8. khaki (42): _____
9. betrayed (47): _____
10. imperceptibly (48): _____
11. therapy (56): _____
12. reverberated (62): _____
13. dilemma (77): _____
14. haphazard (86): _____
15. conspiracy (92): _____

Many words evoke certain feelings in readers depending on the
readers' past experiences or associations. For the following words,
write a one- or two-word reaction.

1. crazy house (1): _____
2. greaseball (4): _____
3. dictator (15): _____
4. purgatory (17): _____
5. Jewish (25): _____
6. Nazis (37): _____
7. Hitler (38): _____
8. Auschwitz (38): _____

FIGURE 3–1 *Word Study*

Reader Response and Discussion

Readers can make better sense of their response to a piece of literature if they record that response in writing. To encourage critical thinking, Traci gives students a series of questions to be answered as they read each chapter of *Tunes*, then she collects all responses after completion of the novel. For example, for chapter 1, she asks students to make inferences about Mr. Hairston:

> Mr. Hairston made negative comments regarding some of his customers. Why do you think he does this? How would his customers respond if they knew how he spoke? Why doesn't Henry say anything to Mr. Hairston about his remarks?

One student, Kerri, responds matter-of-factly:

> Mr. Hairston says this because he is racist and looks for the negative in people instead of the positive. Customers would probably never come back to his store if they knew what he was saying about them. Henry doesn't say anything because he doesn't want to lose his job.

Delving a bit more deeply into Mr. Hairston's motivation, Celia writes:

> [Mr. Hairston] says these things because he is insecure about himself and his own qualities. If he picks out everyone else's imperfections, he feels his aren't as visible. If just one customer found out about his comments, they would spread the word to the rest of the town and everyone would no longer shop at his store. Henry is intimidated by the comments and figures that if he stays out of [Mr. Hairston's] way, he will stay on his good side. [Mr. Hairston] might not say anything about him if he likes him.

Later, as their reading of the novel progresses to chapter 18, Traci asks students perhaps the most difficult question, tapping their analytical, interpretive, and evaluative skills and inviting a personal connection:

> Did Henry destroy Mr. Levine's village? Did he intend to destroy it? How

did he feel after it was destroyed? What would you have done if you were in Henry's position?

Cassie replies:

> Henry does end up destroying Mr. Levine's village. In a way I don't think he really meant to destroy it, but then if he did not mean to, why did he come to do it in the first place? He [didn't have] to go and hurt a friend like that. After he destroyed the village he felt terrible. If I was him I would have never [gone] in the first place and would have [gone] home and told my mom.

Almost all of the students felt that Henry did not intend to destroy Mr. Levine's village. They believed he was frightened by the rat jumping on the table and dropped the hammer accidentally. But Cassie was not quite comfortable with letting Henry off that easily, wondering why he went to the craft center at all if he didn't intend to do the destruction. This chapter is one of the most discussion-rich in the novel and worth more prodding on the part of the teacher to encourage a deeper look at Henry's motivation.

Traci's questions range from tapping simple recall skills to assessing student comprehension, interpretation, analysis, and evaluation (see Figure 3–2). Inviting students to respond in a journal-like format and allowing them to discuss their answers in class is a nonthreatening way to assess both their reading and understanding of the novel.

Character Study

Students seem to respond well to charting behavior, so Traci approaches character study by having her students chart personality traits of certain characters as they appear both at the beginning and the end of the novel (see Figure 3–3). Because students sometimes confuse personality with appearance, Traci cautions them not to include appearance in their list.

One benefit of this assignment is the opportunity to examine character growth and change throughout the story. It's an excellent chance to

Tunes for Bears to Dance To
Discussion Questions

Answer the following questions on a separate sheet of paper as you read each chapter. Responses should be written neatly in cursive using blue or black ink. Write on one side of the page only. All responses should be labeled by chapter number. All twenty responses will be collected upon the novel's completion.

Chapter 1: Mr. Hairston made negative comments regarding some of his customers. Why do you think he does this? How would his customers respond if they knew how he spoke? Why doesn't Henry say anything to Mr. Hairston about his remarks?

Chapter 2: Why did Henry follow Mr. Levine from the crazy house to the building? What do you predict Mr. Levine was doing inside the place and what was in his black bag?

Chapter 3: Henry sees Doris, Mr. Hairston's daughter, for the first time. How does she react to seeing him? What is her physical appearance? Why does he pray for her that night?

Chapter 4: Explain why Henry learns about Mr. Levine's past from George Graham. Why is it important that Mr. Levine gave Henry a carved duck?

Chapter 5: Why would Henry's mother think their old neighborhood would hold "too many memories"? Why did they return to their former town, Monument? How does each member of the family cope with Eddie's death?

Chapter 6: Why was Henry surprised by the fact that Mr. Hairston volunteered to talk to Barstow? Would you expect Mr. Hairston to do this? Why or why not? Will Mr. Hairston expect anything in return?

Chapter 7: What did the Nazis do to Mr. Levine's village? How did this affect his reaction to seeing blood? Is this the reaction you would expect?

Chapter 8: How did Henry react to Jackie Antonelli's comment about his father? What are some nonviolent ways he could have responded to Jackie?

(*continues*)

FIGURE 3–2 *Discussion Questions*

Chapter 9: Why did Henry think he betrayed Mr. Levine by telling Mr. Hairston about the village?

Chapter 10: What do readers learn about Doris? How could Henry's friendship help Doris?

Chapter 11: Why does Henry decide not to tell his mother about the monument for Eddie yet? What do you think Mr. Hairston meant when he told Henry, "Maybe we can work something out"?

Chapter 12: Where does Henry's father go? Why? How does Henry react to this news?

Chapter 13: Why was there an X marked across the sketch of the monument? Why will Henry be fired at the end of the week?

Chapter 14: What happened to Mr. Levine that made Henry forget his problems for a short while? How did Mr. Levine make an effort to include Henry in his life?

Chapter 15: Mr. Hairston enjoyed making his customers wait during the war, "I'd make them line up. Make them wait, acting like the stuff hadn't arrived yet but was expected any minute. All the time the order was here and they waited in line. I was like a dictator, the way they treated me. I *was* a dictator." What does he do to get control over Henry about the monument?

Chapter 16: Why did Mr. Hairston want Mr. Levine's village to be destroyed?

Chapter 17: How does Mr. Hairston play on Henry's feelings about his mother to try to control him?

Chapter 18: Did Henry destroy Mr. Levine's village? Did he intend to destroy it? How did he feel after it was destroyed? What would you have done if you were in Henry's position?

Chapter 19: Why won't Henry accept the rewards for smashing the village? What did he mean when he thought, "It was me he was after all the time. Not just the old man and his village"?

Chapter 20: Why did Henry's family move back to Frenchtown? Describe the last conversation Henry had with Doris. How did Mr. Levine react after learning that his village was destroyed? Why does Henry end the book by asking forgiveness for both himself and Mr. Hairston?

FIGURE 3–2 *Discussion Questions*

Tunes for Bears to Dance To
Character Study Chart

For each character, list personality traits from the beginning to the end of the novel. Do not include appearance.

Jason	Trent	Sarah	Alicia	Brad

FIGURE 3–3 *Character Study Chart*

introduce the terms *static, dynamic, round,* and *flat* in relation to character and to explore the effects that the actions of one character may have on another. Students can learn terms such as *protagonist* and *antagonist* and connect them immediately to Henry and Mr. Hairston, rather than learning them in isolation as literary terminology. They can learn that, though Doris (Mr. Hairston's daughter) and Mr. Levine are minor characters in the novel, they have a significant influence on Henry's emotional and psychological growth.

Independent Projects

To encourage student creativity, Traci also offers them the opportunity to do independent projects related to *Tunes*. The first project deals with point of view, inviting students to retell the story through the eyes of another character (see Figure 3–4). The second alternative is based on a multigenre approach, giving students the chance to build and present to the class a diorama of a scene or scenes from the novel.

In response to the first assignment, Emma takes on the persona of Mr. Levine and writes:

> As I walked out of the crazy house, I felt someone watching me. I decided to ignore whoever it was. My stride remained steady as I strolled down the sidewalk. Suddenly, a flash of blue caught my eye. I stopped walking as I remembered the blue dress my youngest daughter used to wear every Sunday. My hand tipped my hat without me telling it to, and I snapped out of my daze. Then, I continued on to the craft center.
>
> Once inside, I headed straight for my bench. I stared at my small village for a moment, and then I picked up the unfinished carving of my son. I carefully carved his bright eyes and quick smile.
>
> I carved there until George Graham called for us to clean up. Sometimes it was hard to leave my village. It was full of memories both good and bad. When I finish, it will look like my real village before the Nazis came.
>
> I walked home slowly and was relieved when I didn't feel the eyes staring at me. My bed at the crazy house was a comfort to my aching bones. I

Tunes for Bears to Dance To
Independent Projects

Project 1 (In class)
Retell the story through the eyes of a character other than Henry. Choose from Mr. Hairston, Mr. Levine, Doris, Henry's mother, Henry's father, or the ghost of Eddie. Because not all characters are familiar with all the dilemmas Henry faces, focus only on those in which that character is familiar. This should be written using first-person narration. (Put yourself in the character's position; use *I* as you tell the story.) For example, you may write about Mr. Levine's past and how he came to live in the crazy house, how and why he sought comfort in rebuilding his village, why he took an interest in Henry, and his feelings when he won the award and when his wooden village was destroyed. You would also discuss why he chose to rebuild it.

You will have the class period to create a rough draft of the assignment. Rough drafts will be collected at the end of the period. They will be returned for revision into a final draft. Rough drafts will be worth 15 points. Final drafts will be worth 50 points.

Project 2 (Out of class)
Mr. Levine takes great pride in re-creating his village from wood carvings. Using a shoebox (or other box of similar size), re-create either a scene from the novel or a scene from your own "village" or neighborhood. Objects used should be three-dimensional. You may also draw houses or include pictures, if you have room. For example, if kids in your neighborhood always play ball in the backyard, you may want to include a small ball (the kind you would use when playing jacks). When you were younger, if you played hopscotch, draw a hopscotch court on the "ground" of your neighborhood. The diorama should include at least eight items pertaining to the novel or your neighborhood.

Be prepared to briefly explain your diorama to the class. Projects will be worth 25 points.

FIGURE 3–4 *Independent Projects*

was grateful for the darkness. In the concentration camps, the Nazis had always used flashlights, and we could tell when they were coming. My dreams were filled with piles of dead corpses and my little girls were drowning in blood. I woke up screaming and soaked in sweat. I laid in bed shivering until morning.

When I left the house, I didn't feel anyone watching me. I hoped they had gone away. Then, I saw a boy out of the corner of my eye. He was following me. I hid in an empty alleyway to wait for him to pass.

The boy edged slowly toward me as he soothed in a soft voice, "I'm not going to hurt you." He blushed and explained, "I've been watching you. I broke my leg and my brother . . . he's dead."

I felt tears travel down my cheeks. He looked just like my son, and he had lost someone, too. I could understand what he was saying, but I had trouble forming [my] words. "Dead?" I choked out.

He nodded solemnly and touched my shoulder. I decided to bring him to see my village. "Come," I said as I motioned for him to follow me. As we approached the craft center, we saw George pacing on the sidewalk.

"Are you all right? Did he scare you?" George asked in Yiddish.

"I'm fine. I want to show you something," I replied in the same language. George nodded thoughtfully.

I led the boy to my bench and showed him the wooden village. I watched his eyes widen and his jaw drop. My carved people looked alive.

As the boy seated himself, I whittled a small duck from a block of balsa wood. I handed it to him and he gazed at it in wonder. The boy watched me work for awhile; then, he thanked me for the duck and left. I hoped he would come back.

A few days passed before he returned. I asked George to tell the boy I wanted to teach him how to carve. The boy looked unsure, but George managed to persuade him. I positioned his hands around the knife and wood. Then, I guided him through the first few strokes. Suddenly, the knife slipped and cut his finger. I quickly tied it up, but my stomach lurched at the sight of blood. George was next to me in a second.

He explained to the boy why I had fainted. The Nazis had turned my village into a concentration camp. My wife and two daughters were sent to another camp called Auschwitz. My son died the first winter after they came. I was only one of the few that had survived. I heard them talking, but it seemed from a distance. George explained that I tipped my hat because the guards would beat me if I didn't. After that, the boy left with pained eyes.

Two days later, George ran up to me as I walked toward the center. He held a letter above his head like a banner.

"You won first prize! The best work of art!" George exclaimed as he laughed at my wide-eyed expression. I stared at him in shock. When we entered the center, a roar of applause greeted us.

The boy arrived looking discouraged, but brightened when he heard the good news. I smiled; it was like my son was there with me.

"You're a good boy," I said slowly in English, "Invite . . . invite." I looked to George for help.

"Oh, he wants to invite you to the ceremony. Saturday afternoon. At two o'clock," he explained.

"You come?" I asked hopefully.

The boy nodded and glanced at the carved village lovingly. Then, some of the ladies at the center brought a huge white cake. I remembered the cakes my mother used to bake and grinned.

After the party was over, I pulled a small bottle and cloth out of my bag. Then, I gently polished all of my carvings until they seemed to glow. The boy left with a lighter step that afternoon, and I pictured his smile.

Once I returned to the house, I carefully carved the figure of a boy. Then, I added a pair of dancing eyes with a smile that lit up his whole face. I slipped it under my pillow and promised I would finish it later. I slept soundly through the night.

The next morning, I [went] happily to the craft center. I entered and felt the floor jerk away from under my feet. George steadied me and tried to comfort me with soothing words. My [village] had been destroyed.

I hurried over to my bench and searched for my family. I let out a slow sigh of relief when I found they they had only been knocked over. I could survive this.

First, I found the figure of the boy in my bag and finished it. Then, I started recreating the barn. I placed my memories into the wood with every stroke.

The boy didn't come back for three weeks. I didn't notice him until he sat down next to me. He gazed mournfully at my half-repaired village.

George told me that the boy was moving [away]. Hope filled me and I embraced the boy. "Wait," I whispered and dug into my bag until I felt the carved figure. I placed it in his hand. He smiled and I knew he would keep it forever. When he left that day, I could finally let my son go with him.

About this assignment, Traci says:

Our character discussion lends itself to [this] assignment. . . . Most students tend to focus on Mr. Levine, since we already know a little bit of his history from the story itself. I have also read some good papers where students write about Mr. Hairston being poor, abused, and always hungry as a child, which partly explains his greed, need for control, and abuse of his own wife and daughter.

About teaching the novel, she adds:

This novel also promotes critical thinking and enhances students' predicting skills. Because Henry has several decisions to make throughout the novel, it allows students to think about what consequences their actions have and how these actions may affect others. They always try to guess whether or not Henry will tell his mother that he is being blackmailed, whether or not he will go through with smashing the wooden village, and whether or not Mr. Hairston will be publicly exposed for his treachery.

Review for Final Test

Rather than give her seventh graders an objective test on the novel, Traci takes the opportunity to review for the final essay test by giving the students a study sheet comprised of ten questions, which they must answer to assist in their understanding of the book:

1. Explain the following quote by Gustave Flaubert and how it relates to the title and themes of the novel: "Human language is like a cracked kettle on which we beat tunes for bears to dance to, when all the time we are longing to move the stars to pity."

2. Explain why Henry quotes "The Lord's Prayer" throughout this novel, especially at the end, when he whispers, "Deliver us from evil."

3. Are the decisions we make always black or white? The rewards offered by Mr. Hairston do not come without a cost to Henry. Even though he doesn't take the physical rewards, how do his actions affect him?

4. One of the novel's themes is about the conflict between good versus evil. Who has "won" the conflict? Do you feel that anyone is a true winner?

5. Provide two examples for each of the following themes from the novel: manipulation, loss of innocence, prejudice/racism.

6. Mr. Hairston says, "You only appreciate something when you think you have lost it." Is this true? How could Mr. Hairston have shown empathy for the other characters?

7. Longfellow wrote, "If we could read the secret history of our enemies, we would find in each man's life a sorrow and suffering enough to disarm all hostility." Does this apply to Mr. Hairston or any of the other characters?

8. Provide one example of each type of conflict in the novel: character vs. character, character vs. self, character vs. nature, character vs. fate, character vs. society.

9. Explain the parts of the novel's plot: exposition, rising action, climax, falling action, resolution.

10. Why did Mr. Hairston hate Mr. Levine so much and want his village destroyed? How did Mr. Hairston also destroy Henry?

To question 3, Sara responds:

> [Our decisions] are not always right or wrong. Henry feels awful about what he did to Mr. Levine's village. He did it for the rewards, and you can somewhat connect a quote from "The Lord's Prayer": "Lead us not into temptation," meaning keep us from doing bad things even if a reward is given.

Similarly, Amy writes:

> [Henry's] actions affect him [because] he destroyed the village, and he has to live with that guilt. Some of our decisions aren't always right or wrong. Even though Henry didn't take the rewards, he still destroyed the village. He didn't take the rewards because he was ashamed, and he wanted to make himself feel better.

Both of these responses demonstrate insight into Henry's guilt at his destructive act, giving Traci a good idea of these students' understanding of this underlying theme in the novel and helping the students come to terms with their own thinking on the matter. Review questions such as these probe important issues in the novel, encouraging students to think more critically *before* taking the final test and increasing their chances of a successful result.

Cormier's Reflections on the Novel

In an interview with Mitzi Myers (2000), Robert Cormier talked about his motivation for writing *Tunes for Bears to Dance To*:

> I do believe, sincerely, that we are all made up of the good and the bad, that we have as much capacity for evil as for good but a certain moral fiber steers us away from the evil. Some people are untested simply because they have lacked the opportunity not to be good. (454) . . . I didn't set out to write a "Holocaust Novel" with *Tunes for Bears to Dance To*, but the Holocaust was very much on my mind. I'd been reading about it, and of all the horrors that I ran across what struck me the most were the little horrors, the small things that haunt at midnight. The compulsive reactions, like the old man tipping his hat. . . . About the same time, a woodcarver

friend of mine displayed his latest creation at a local arts and crafts show. His centerpiece was the re-creation of his hometown village in Canada . . . It was a masterpiece, so detailed and lovingly made. People brushed casually by the table on which it was displayed and where it remained on display for three days and nights. It seemed to be very vulnerable and almost welcoming an accident that would damage or destroy it. . . . I remembered a grocer I ran errands for when I was nine or ten years old. He seemed to be a nice guy, but he was a practical joker. And his jokes, which he played on me and another boy, sometimes crossed the line between fun and cruelty. To go into detail would take up too much space, but let me say that one particular "joke" left me utterly humiliated, and it has remained with me through the years. Somehow it came back to me as I was pondering what to do about the woodcarver's village and the hat compulsion. (457–58)

The Teaching

At 101 pages, *Tunes for Bears to Dance To* is one of Robert Cormier's shortest novels. Yet, as one of my students pointed out, it is packed with important issues to consider and discuss, issues that explore our very being and moral fiber. As Traci O'Brian and her students have shown, this novel can be a valuable addition to the middle school curriculum. And, as my graduate students have demonstrated by finding the book compelling enough to discuss for hours and wishing for more time to explore it further, this is a novel for everyone. That universal appeal separates truly good literature from mediocre stories directed to a particular audience. To paraphrase C. S. Lewis, if a writer has a story to tell, he or she should tell it in the best, most skillful, way possible, and it will find its own audience. There is no need to talk down to children or young adults. They are sharp enough to recognize condescension when they see it. Robert Cormier knows this, as he has said repeatedly, "I write for the intelligent reader, regardless of that reader's age."

The Rag and Bone Shop
Truths That Shape the Soul

Readers of Robert Cormier's novels know they are not for the faint-hearted, even though his books are marketed to a young adult audience. (As we have seen, Cormier has repeatedly denied the assumption that he writes for readers of a certain age.) As with all of Cormier's novels, some adult readers of *The Rag and Bone Shop* find it too disturbing for young adults, as it examines the psychological manipulation of an innocent boy by an adult determined to advance himself professionally at the boy's expense.

The trouble begins when seven-year-old Alicia Bartlett is found murdered in a wooded area near her home. She is a neighbor and friend of twelve-year-old Jason Dorrant, the protagonist in the story, and he is supposedly the last person to have seen her before her death. As the investigation into her murder progresses, the townspeople become anxious for the killer to be caught, and police are pressured by a local senator to solve the case. Desperate for a solution, Detective Lieutenant George Braxton, who is in charge of the investigation, convinces himself that Jason is his prime suspect and solicits the help of an interrogator named Trent, who has a reputation for extracting confessions from even the toughest criminals. Trent's interrogation of Jason comprises much of the novel, leading to a surprising and disturbing ending.

Adults who fear that this novel is too shocking for adolescent readers may underestimate the resilience of young people, as protective adults often do. The reaction of Traci O'Brian's seventh-grade students to this novel, however, demonstrates their ability to understand and explore its sophisticated themes of innocence, betrayal, and redemption.

On her reasons for teaching the novel, Traci explains:

> I teach *The Rag and Bone Shop* after the students read *Tunes for Bears to Dance To*. It is quite a shock for them to start this book immediately after *Tunes* because the writing style is more sophisticated and the plot itself is much more graphic and shocking. In Part One of this novel, the murder of a family, including a young boy, is described in some detail. This shock within the first few pages definitely motivates the students to keep reading.
>
> We begin the study of this novel by discussing the title and cover illustration. Of course, no seventh grader has ever guessed that the title comes from a line in the Yeats poem, "The Circus Animals' Desertion," but some students say the fact that Jason's body is half light and half dark [on the cover] shows that there are two sides to his personality—maybe an innocent and an evil side.

Unlike with teaching *Tunes for Bears to Dance To*, Traci does not give her students a final test on this novel, only a few short writing assignments that encourage them to interpret the story. Defending her decision not to test the students, she continues:

> Every single student each year has written (through anonymous surveys) that he or she did in fact finish the book, and in some cases, this was the only book he or she had ever read in its entirety.
>
> We do briefly discuss literary elements, but we also talk about the characters and the motivations for their actions. We talk about why Lottie [Trent's deceased wife] didn't approve of [Trent's] obsession with his career; we talk about why Jason wanted to create a suspect just so he could feel involved in the investigation; and we talk about why Brad [Alicia's older brother] killed Alicia in the first place.

Discussion Questions

Traci asks her students to select four of the following discussion questions and respond to them in writing, assessing their understanding of the story and encouraging them to think critically about the novel:

- After Jason hits Bobo Kelton, "he didn't think he'd ever hit anybody again but he had proved himself capable of doing it" (26). How does the second part of that sentence become a weapon later for Trent? Why does hitting Bobo mean an end to Jason's tears? Is the principal right when he says that violence never solves anything?

- Trent's wife Lottie had told him, "You are what you do." Why does this make Trent feel bad or guilty? Is it true that people are what they do, not only in their jobs, but in their lives? Can this be changed?

- Sarah Downes and Carl Seaton compare Trent to a priest. How are Trent's interrogations similar to what a priest does in the confessional? What differences are there between Trent and a priest?

- What are the heavy external and internal pressures on Trent to get a confession from Jason? In real life, is it possible that this kind of pressure may result in wrongly convicting innocent people? What might be done to keep this from happening?

- Trent says he has "rules and regulations" for interrogations. What are some of these strategies that relate to the physical setup of the room and Jason's intimidation? How do these interrogation techniques affect the suspect?

- As Trent questions Jason, he suddenly realizes that Jason is innocent. How does he talk himself out of releasing Jason? What would have been the consequences if he had allowed himself to let Jason go? Did Trent do the right thing?

- A plot twist takes us by surprise when Trent emerges into the hall after Jason has "confessed" and is told the truth by Sarah Downes. Suddenly, everything is different. What could happen to Trent and Jason?

- In the end, Jason's view of reality has been twisted by Trent's questioning and his own actions. What does he tell himself to justify his plan to kill Bobo? How will this action restore his self-respect?

To the third question, comparing Trent to a priest in the confessional, Eric writes:

> In a confessional, the priest listens to your confession to a sin. Trent's job is much like a priest's job because he, too, must listen to confessions. One of the main differences is that a priest can give absolution and Trent cannot. Another difference is that people decide to confess to the priest because their heart tells them to. Trent, however, ensnares the suspect into a trap to get them to confess, whether they're guilty or not.

Question number four, about external and internal pressures, elicits this response from Brianna:

> Trent has more external pressures to get Jason to confess than internal ones. One is that Trent does not want to look bad for letting Jason go free. Another pressure is that the [senator] has offered Trent the ability to do whatever he wants if Jason confesses. The last pressure is that families want to sleep easily and will be angry if he can't find the killer. The internal pressure is Trent's ego. He doesn't want to look bad and he wants to get a better job. These pressures can definitely cause wrong convictions because Trent would be more interested in furthering his career, which would lead to false convictions and trials. I think the only way to keep this from happening is to make sure real evidence is present before accusing people of crimes.

The last question, perhaps the most intriguing of all, relates to the effect the interrogation and confession have had on Jason. Daria responds:

> In the end, Jason's views of reality and fantasy have been twisted. Trent's interrogation seriously damaged Jason's way of thinking. Jason thinks that if he says he can kill someone, maybe he really could. He plans to kill Bobo, a bully; doing this will gain back Jason's self-respect. Jason will show himself and everyone else that he is not a coward, and he can defend himself. He feels that he needs to prove that he is capable of causing havoc and chaos. Killing Bobo is kind of like giving Jason a voice.

Daria's comment about giving Jason a voice is insightful, though she seems to miss the point that admitting to a crime he didn't commit may have actually turned him into a murderer. Still, her response warrants further class discussion about Jason's decision to kill Bobo and whether he will actually go through with it.

Common to all these responses is an insight that belies some assumptions about the ability of seventh graders to think critically about literature. These students go beyond Jason's actions to his possible motivation for behaving as he does and to the psychological damage that results from the interrogation by Trent. As these students demonstrate, given the right intellectual stimulation by a knowledgeable teacher, they can (and will) go beyond the literal plot events of a story and delve into interpretation and analysis, often discovering insights they didn't realize they had.

In-Class Writing

In addition to the written answers to discussion questions, one of the in-class writing assignments that Traci gives her students is the opportunity to explore the character of Trent, the interrogator. When they have almost finished the novel, she asks them to write their thoughts about Trent, prompting them with the following questions but emphasizing that they are not limited to answering these questions:

- What do you believe are the characteristics of a villain? Who are some of the villains with whom you are familiar (world leaders, entertainers, characters in books or movies, etc.)? Does Trent have these characteristics? Does he consider himself a villain? Did Lottie? Does Jason?

- What do you believe is an appropriate punishment for Trent trying to force a confession from Jason? Does he feel guilty about what he is trying to do? Why does he want Jason to confess?

- What do you believe might have happened in Trent's past to make him an interrogator determined only to obtain a confession, not necessarily the truth? Do you believe that Trent will be successful in getting Jason to confess? What will happen to him if he is successful? What will happen to him if he is unsuccessful?

Though many of the students did respond briefly by more or less answering these questions in order, some tried to look into Trent's character a little more deeply. Carrie, for example, wrote this:

Trent is a middle-aged man [who] has become a loner over time. This probably is because of his wife, Lottie's, death and hearing so much terrorizing and scary confessions. Although he isn't the kindest person, I wouldn't describe him as a villain. Villains are very evil, have some sort of reason for not liking someone in particular. One characteristic I do notice is that he is a bit villainous in his ability to frighten and discourage. When I hear the word *villain*, I automatically think of Disney characters. Captain Hook, the queen in Sleeping Beauty, and Ursula from the Little Mermaid are my generation's classic stereotypes. [Trent] doesn't perceive himself as evil (I think not at all) and neither did Lottie or Jason. Both of these characters do recognize, though, his unavoidable coldness.

Trent doesn't think he is going too far in the interrogation and forgets that Jason still may not understand what they are accusing him of doing. Therefore, I believe he should have toned [it] down. I also believe he doesn't work well with younger people. He is intimidating and doesn't know how to be very gentle. As punishment, even though this truly is just a restriction, he should [question only] adults [whom] the police have already identified as the perpetrator and not just a guess. He only cares about his reputation, which is why he is practically forcing [the confession] out of [Jason]. Maybe he should take a break from this job until he can come back and worry about the truth and doing the right thing instead of himself and his reputation. He isn't a bad person, just someone [who] got lost between job and life, right and wrong, and fame and love.

While a few of Traci's students agreed with Carrie that Trent is not a villain, but rather a misguided adult who needs help, most of them condemned him as villainous, comparing him to the likes of Saddam Hussein and Valdemoort of the Harry Potter series. Of the novel itself, one student, Kenny, notes, "*The Rag and Bone Shop* is an excellent book so far. I can't wait to see if Trent will get Jason to confess." Then, making a prediction, he adds, "I think he will get Jason to confess, although I think Jason is innocent." Kenny's comment seems to underscore Cormier's concern about the abuse of adult power over young people, since Kenny is resigned to Jason's tragic fate, even though he knows Jason is innocent. This kind of response marks a teachable moment, when students can be encouraged to think further about the issue of adult power and what, if anything, can be done to prevent its abuse.

Interestingly, though all the students feel that Jason is innocent of killing Alicia, they are quite matter-of-fact about Trent's tactics in extracting Jason's confession. None of the responses expresses outrage or sorrow at Jason's fate—or horror at his decision in the end to kill Bobo Kelton. Kenny's excitement about the book's ending is the closest anyone comes to a personal response. While the students' writing certainly indicates engagement with the story, their distance from the characters as *people* is a bit puzzling. Perhaps because this is a school assignment, they don't feel free to express their emotions about Jason's fate, or perhaps they feel it's just not "cool" to let emotions show. Traci comments: "The favorite part for students, of course, is the ending, where Jason takes the butcher knife and plans to wait for Bobo Kelton. I overhear students talking in the halls saying, 'You'll never believe how it ends!'" Perhaps to these seventh graders this book is no different from many of today's movies, where violent behavior is no longer shocking but exciting. Another teachable moment?

Book Jacket Design Project

To encourage further thought by her students of the events in *The Rag and Bone Shop*, Traci uses a book jacket design project, in which students are asked to come up with a new appropriate title for the novel, design a cover to fit the title, write a blurb for the back cover, and explain why they've chosen this new title and cover. Daria, for example, changed the book's title to *Shallow Innocence*, featuring a large knife on the cover surrounded by names and peering eyes (see Figure 4–1). She explains:

> The reason for the blade on the cover is to show Jason's new way of thinking. The blade represents power and uncontrolled emotions [that] Jason is now feeling. As you notice, that isn't blood dripping off the knife; they are tears. Jason made a promise to himself that he would never cry again. When he can't let his emotions out with tears, he lets out his bottled up

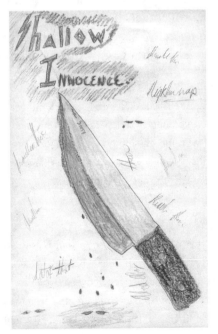

FIGURE 4–1 *Shallow Innocence*

anger with a knife in the end of the story. The names on the cover represent the victims of Trent's actions, the people that could have died because of him. The eyes on the cover represent the way Trent made [Jason] feel; the eyes that were constantly staring him down, the same eyes that drove Jason, literally, insane.

The reasoning behind the title *Shallow Innocence* is to explain two people in the story. *Shallow* to tell Trent's story; during the interrogation Trent was very shallow. He put himself before Jason. *Innocence* is Jason. He was innocent the whole time and still is. The word *shallow* is above *innocence* [on the cover] because Trent overpowered Jason.

Daria's back cover blurb is short and succinct:

Jason is a misread teen. He is accused of the most awful crime possible. Is he innocent? It takes a genius to find out if Jason is capable of killing a seven-year-old friend.

Eric took a different approach, focusing on the puzzle aspect of the story. His cover is almost entirely black, with the title, *Puzzle of a Murder,* and the author's name in two shades of purple (see Figure 4–2). In the center is a white puzzle with a girl's figure superimposed over it. Eric says of his choices:

I chose the title because Alicia liked puzzles, and a murder story is like one giant puzzle. The background is black because this is a dark book. I chose the picture of the girl with the missing puzzle piece for a head because Alicia liked puzzles, and you cannot see her face because Jason couldn't tell what Alicia was really like after the questioning.

For the back cover blurb, Eric writes:

Jason is a twelve-year-old boy who is a social outcast, someone who's there but isn't. Jason hangs out with Alicia Bartlett, a seven-year-old. On Monday, she was found dead wedged between two trees. Jason was at her house shortly before she was murdered. Trent is an interrogator bent on doing one thing, getting Jason to confess, whether he is guilty or not.

A third student, Daniel, was interested in the two sides of Jason's

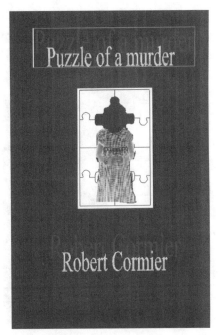

FIGURE 4–2 *Puzzle of a Murder*

personality. Titling the book *Guilty or Innocent?* he wrote the word *Guilty?* in large block letters at the top of the page, while *Innocent?* appears in much smaller lowercase letters beneath it (see Figure 4–3). Dividing the cover into two vertical sections, Daniel gave the left section a white background, drawing a puzzle piece and a mystery book on the side he labeled *light*. The right section of the cover is black, showing a large knife dripping blood under the word *dark*. Daniel rationalizes:

> I picked this title because Trent wants to know if Jason is guilty or innocent
> . . . during the interrogation. The picture is of Jason's two sides—his dark
> side and light side. They show what he does when he shows the two dif-
> ferent sides [of his personality].

To entice the reader, Daniel's back cover blurb reads:

> Jason Dorrant, twelve years old, was the last one to see poor Alicia alive.
> Jason was good friends with Alicia, and they were always nice to each

FIGURE 4–3 *Guilty? Or Innocent?*

other. But one day Jason left her house, and she was dead in the next hour. Did Jason do it? Trent the interrogator would soon find out!

Each of these three students takes a different perspective on the story. Daria is more concerned with Jason's innocence and the change that comes over him after the interrogation. She concentrates especially on his vow never to cry again and how this decision may have been responsible for his resolve to kill Bobo Kelton. Her cover demonstrates some real critical thinking, as she analyzes and synthesizes various aspects of the story in her representation. Eric, on the other hand, seems more interested in the connection between Alicia's penchant for solving puzzles and the puzzling mystery of her death. His stark cover is powerful in its rendering of the crux of the story. Similarly, his back cover blurb tells prospective readers just enough to entice them into the book. Finally, Daniel is obviously thinking about the dichotomy so prevalent in all of Cormier's books: the struggle between good and evil. Details from the story are evident all over the cover, from the puzzle piece that reflects

Jason and Alicia's innocent relationship, to the generic mystery novel that represents Jason's reading preference, which is later used as evidence against him, to the blood-dripping knife that predicts the outcome of Trent's interrogation of Jason. Even the size and shape of the title letters send a message about the novel's contents.

Traci's use of this multigenre approach as part of the study of *The Rag and Bone Shop* taps her students' artistic and linguistic intelligence, resulting in a better sense of their comprehension of the novel. It's a safe bet that the students themselves discovered more about their response to the story through this assignment, since it encouraged them to emphasize what they felt was important about the novel and its characters.

Censorship and *The Rag and Bone Shop*

As with all of Robert Cormier's novels, *The Rag and Bone Shop* has its share of detractors, most of whom are adults who fear the novel's effect on young readers. Teachers who use the book are always open to criticism, and, unfortunately, Traci didn't escape the wrath of the censors. She describes her experience:

> I read Part One aloud to my students, where the murder of a young family is described while Carl Seaton confesses to Trent. When I got to the part about how he pictured the woman without wearing her nightgown, there were a few snickers and chuckles from the back of the room. When I got to the part about how [Seaton] killed the ten-year-old boy out of kindness, I heard gasps. When I finished reading Part One, some students said they liked [the book] so far, but all of them were a little surprised that we were reading this book in school. I informed them that the beginning was one of the most graphic parts of the novel and that the rest of it was mostly about intimidation and manipulation. No one complained either publicly or privately about the book's contents or said they were uncomfortable reading it.
>
> The next morning I received an email from a mother who wrote that when she picked up her son from school the previous afternoon, she could tell something was wrong because he was so quiet. After prodding him, she

learned that he was upset about the book we were reading during class. He didn't like the violence or the references to sex within the first few pages.

She informed me that she actually stayed up that night and read the entire book herself instead of just reading some passages out of context. She was unhappy with the violent content, the brief reference to a sexual thought, and the fact that the protagonist in the end may be a murderer. In her email she asked if she and her husband could meet with me that day before her son had to read any more of the book.

During our conference, I had numerous materials available regarding censorship and even some of Cormier's own statements about censorship being dangerous. Both parents were concerned that the novel was "too real" as far as the evidence was concerned. I explained that was one of my purposes in selecting the novel. The students could relate to Jason and being accused of something they didn't do much more than they could relate to some other characters and situations we read about that year. I told the parents that I choose a variety of literature, and this book was chosen for its suspense and realism.

I explained that I went through the proper channels to have the book approved by the school board, including having two other classroom teachers read it and sign that they approved, and sending copies to the director of curriculum and the school board. I also wrote a formal request to teach the book, as well as a rationale (which is not ever required or standard practice), and I submitted these to the school board because I anticipated some objections. The book was unanimously approved. The parents questioned whether anyone actually read it or just blindly approved it. I told them that I couldn't speak for the school board, but the director of curriculum actually wrote me a personal note saying how much he enjoyed reading a new Cormier novel. (He was my former sophomore English teacher.) The parents didn't approve of that comment.

I offered other novels for their son to read as an alternative, but they took issue with each one I selected after reading commentaries and summaries on the Internet. Finally, I told them that if they could find a noncontroversial young adult novel in the realistic fiction genre, I would let their son read it and write a literary analysis paper on it. They couldn't find one that they approved of, so they let him continue reading *The Rag and Bone Shop*, proclaiming that the damage was already done.

The final email from the mother stated that she was very disappointed in me and that she always thought I was a more caring and sensitive teacher. This was a surprising comment because I had taught her two other children in previous years and have gotten to know her personally through her involvement in volunteering at the school. Ironically, her other two children read *Tunes for Bears to Dance To*, and her daughter read *The Rag and Bone Shop*, and no one had a problem. [The mother] also stated that she does believe in censorship and thinks that more people should, too.

Since this experience, I send this family an email every time we start a new novel so they can preview it. Surprisingly, there were no objections to the smoking, gangs, or murders in *The Outsiders* or the "nightmen" burning and framing African American characters for crimes they didn't commit in *Roll of Thunder, Hear My Cry*.

[The parents] didn't approach my principal, the director of curriculum, or the school board about trying to have this book removed because they said they didn't care about other people's children, only their own. I didn't tell anyone in authority about this issue because I wanted to try to resolve it at my level.

When we finished the novel, I asked students to anonymously submit opinions about the novel's strengths and weaknesses and whether or not they felt this novel was appropriate to be taught in school. Out of the sixty students who read it this year, only one student said that he didn't think it should be read. I assume that this was the student who complained in the first place.

On the flip side of this issue, one father emailed me that he was reading the book along with his son and absolutely loved it, saying that he wished he could have read books like this when he was in school; he might have actually liked reading class.

Though Traci didn't enlist the help of administrators or professional organizations in dealing with this censorship attempt, she was prepared for objections to the novel that might arise. Having other teachers read and approve the book, providing copies to administrators and the school board, writing a rationale, and filing a formal request with the school board to teach the book were all wise decisions on her part.

The Final Novel

As Robert Cormier's last novel, *The Rag and Bone Shop* evokes a certain sadness that transcends even the tragic events of the story. In her article, "The Last Cormier," published in *Horn Book*'s "Sand in the Oyster" column, Patty Campbell (2001) captures the feeling of loss that so many of us felt upon Cormier's death, as she recounts her experience reading the manuscript titled "The Rag and Bone Shop" that lay on her desk soon after he passed away. She tells of her anticipation and her reluctance to begin reading, knowing this would be the last time she would "read a new novel from Robert Cormier." Recalling Cormier's reluctance to talk about any book he was working on, she remembers that he told her two years earlier that he was writing a book called "The Interrogator," the title of which he later changed to "Down Where All the Ladders Start," the line from the Yeats poem "The Circus Animals' Desertion" that precedes the line from which Cormier ultimately took his title. Campbell adds:

> Appropriately enough, the couplet illustrates not only the state of mind of the soul-weary interrogator Trent (both pro- and an-tagonist of the novel) but that of Cormier himself, in its insistence on the artist's painful need to commune with the dark places of the human heart. Cormier's last novel is utterly characteristic in this communication with darkness and in its themes of innocence corrupted, political authority misused, sin and confession and forgiveness and guilt—with an undergirding of religious faith and glimmers of hope just offstage.

Reflecting on Cormier's deep religious faith and its relationship to his writing, Campbell (2001) states:

> Questions of faith are inherent in the novels of the devoutly Catholic Cormier, especially the nature of good and evil and their relationship to guilt and forgiveness. As always, he shows us the light by focusing on the shadow that is its consequence. In *The Rag and Bone Shop* he has structured these ideas into the very shape of the narrative, comparing Trent's unholy work to that of a priest, but one who hears confessions to grant not abso-

lution but indictment. The forgiveness he offers is an illusion, and the peace it brings is short-lived. Like a priest, he is weary with all the terrible deeds he has heard, "the unending litany of confessions," but he can find no peace for himself, nor remission for his own sin of betrayal.

And with brilliant insight, Campbell illuminates the struggle that readers experience upon reading the novel's disturbing ending:

> When Jason emerges from the interrogation room, he looks "broken, as if just lifted down from the cross." His ordeal leads not to redemption, but further sin, as he desperately attempts to reconnect with reality by making his false confession true.

Could this ever happen? Would a twelve-year-old be so disturbed by such an experience that he would go out and commit murder? Does Jason really go through with his decision to kill Bobo Kelton? Regretting that she can no longer pick up the phone and ask Cormier for "a neat and comfortable conclusion" to the novel, Campbell says with resignation, "I know that the answer would be, 'What do you think?' Because Robert Cormier in the humility of his greatness always hands it back to us."

Frenchtown Summer
Reflections of Other Cormier Works

I f ever there were a book that gives us clues to the manifestation of Robert Cormier's inner demons in his characters, it's *Frenchtown Summer.* This poignant prose poem recounting a twelve-year-old's painful search for his identity abounds with memories of people who bear striking resemblance to the characters in Cormier's novels—and in his life. Beginning the poem with the words, "That summer in Frenchtown / in the days / when I knew my name / but did not know who I was . . ." (1), Cormier tells us immediately of Eugene's identity confusion, and we sense that he is speaking from experience. Cormier admitted as much in an article he wrote for *English Journal*:

> I was very much aware as I wrote this free-verse story that I was drawing on my own boyhood—people I know, stories I had heard, legends that had fascinated me throughout my life. I instinctively disguised characters and events as I wrote, but I was constantly aware of the autobiographical elements. (2001a, 31)

Though he was aware of the autobiographical elements in

Frenchtown Summer, we can't help but wonder whether Cormier realized he may have been exorcising some inner demons as well. This brief memoir is an ideal selection for classroom reading because it allows us to delve more deeply into other Cormier works and perhaps satisfy our curiosity about the creation of his characters and plots. The book would make a satisfying conclusion to a unit on Robert Cormier.

Fathers and Sons

From the very first page, where Eugene recalls waiting for his father to come home from work each day, we see the yearning in the boy's heart for his father's attention and approval. Students may welcome the opportunity to think of other Cormier characters who have had similar feelings. Jerry Renault of *The Chocolate War*, for example, longs to have a real conversation with his father, who is too wrapped up in grief over his wife's death to see that his son is hurting, too. And Henry Cassavant of *Tunes for Bears to Dance To* struggles to understand the grief of his cata-tonic father, so devastated over his son Eddie's death that he is unable to communicate. Death also plays a role in the father-son relationship of Richy and his dad in Cormier's short story "In the Heat," anthologized in Don Gallo's collection *Sixteen* (Cormier 1984). Richy's mother has died of cancer, and the story takes place as the father and son prepare to attend the funeral. The conversation between the two is heartrending, as they attempt to make sense of their tragedy and at the same time connect with and console each other. Similarly, the tense relationship between Eugene and his father is woven throughout *Frenchtown Summer*, culmi-nating in the touching final chapter. Discussing and writing about these father-son relationships may help students discover the universality of this theme in Cormier's works and recognize it more readily in other works they read. Activities could include:

- After reading *Frenchtown Summer* in common, divide the class into literature circles, with each small group choosing or being assigned one of Cormier's other novels to read, discuss, and compare with the father-son allusions in *Frenchtown Summer*.

Each group could report its findings to the class, opening the door to further discussion.

- Have students read Carl Sandburg's poem, "What Shall He Tell That Son?" Invite them to make connections between the poem and the father-son relationships in *Frenchtown Summer* and other appropriate Cormier works previously mentioned.

- Draw two columns on the board and as a class brainstorm characteristics of fathers and sons. Ask students to write a short essay on how they think these characteristics affect father-son relationships, positively or negatively. After they've written, discuss how these same characteristics come into play in *Frenchtown Summer* and any other Cormier works students have read.

Bullies

Cormier spoke often about being bullied as a child. He talked about the tough guys who waited for him after school to beat him up, and how he was fortunately able to outrun them. Even dogs, he said, liked to bite him. A bully exists in Eugene's world, too, in the person of Ernie Forcier, who delights in making fun of Eugene every chance he gets. Eugene tells of the day he finally got his new glasses, which made the world seem so beautiful to him. Describing "a world suddenly vivid," he marvels at the ant crawling along the sidewalk and the shard of green glass "gleaming like a distant planet / fallen into the gutter." Then Ernie spoils everything by yelling across the street, "Hey, Four Eyes!" (49).

In almost every Cormier novel we find a bully of some sort. Omer LaBatt, the bully in *Fade*, extorts money from weaker classmates and stalks Paul Moreaux relentlessly—until Paul, in his invisible state, beats Omer badly and leaves him writhing in the alley. Sonny Boy in *Tenderness*, though he doesn't prey on Eric Poole so much, becomes the object of Eric's disgust in prison, as he watches the bully torment the more timid prisoners. Bobo Kelton in *The Rag and Bone Shop* furtively molests Jason's female classmates in the halls and pushes

Jason from behind in the cafeteria, causing him to trip and fall. Sparking Jason's anger, Bobo becomes the object of his hatred and, when Jason fights back, ultimately causes Jason to be viewed as aggressive by the interrogator Trent, helping the man build his case against Jason. But the ultimate bully may be Archie Costello of *The Chocolate War* and *Beyond the Chocolate War*. His brand of psychological intimidation is far more dangerous and lasting than any physical beating, and Cormier makes the most of it in the novel, showing us Archie's effect on not only Jerry Renault, but on many other characters in the book—even the headmaster, Brother Leon. Cormier comments on his obsession with bullies by conveying Eric's thoughts in *Tenderness*: "There was always a bully on the premises, no matter where you went. Bullies in the schoolyard, in the school corridors, on the athletic fields" (71). No one knows the truth of this statement better than our students, many of whom have suffered at the hands of bullies. The subject certainly merits examination, and Cormier's novels provide that opportunity. Following are some questions or activities for discussion or writing, beginning with personal experience and extending to analysis of Cormier's characters:

- How would you define the word *bully*?

- Based on your definition, what bullies have you encountered in your life?

- How did these bullies behave, and how did you react to their behavior?

- Which of Robert Cormier's characters would you classify as bullies? Why?

- Cormier's bullies are usually flat, minor characters, yet they do have an effect on the main character in his novels. Choose a bully from one of Cormier's books and explain how that person influences the thoughts and actions of the book's protagonist.

Teachers interested in examining bullying in Cormier's books with their students might also read C. J. Bott's *The Bully in the Book and in the*

Classroom (Rowman and Littlefield, 2004) for further insight into the problem and how to handle it in the classroom.

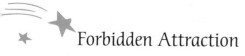

Forbidden Attraction

Eugene thought his mother was beautiful, describing "her eyes the color of bruises / her hair black / as the velvet on which diamonds were displayed" (1999, 22). Emphasizing her gracefulness, he notes that she was not like his "sturdy aunts who stomped off to the comb shops in the mornings / or the vigorous aunts / who stayed home with the babies / scrubbing, ironing / pummeling carpets on clotheslines" (22–23). Readers of Cormier's novel *Tenderness* will recognize this description as the same one the author uses to describe Eric Poole's mother, who, we later find out, may have sexually abused Eric, causing his obsession with killing dark-haired young women in order to find "tenderness." (Cormier masterfully plants this thought in our minds but never quite validates it in the novel.)

Another example of this theme can be found in *Fade* (1988). Cormier had a favorite aunt whom he visited occasionally. Though his love and admiration for her were purely platonic, he fantasizes through his character Paul Moreaux, who is sexually attracted to his Aunt Rosanna and her checkered past. The rumor was that she had gone away to have an illegitimate child, and when she returns to Frenchtown alone, young Paul is curious about her and her relationships with men. When she lets him caress her breast through her silk blouse, he is both delighted and ashamed, swearing his love for her while agonizing over telling the priest of his sin in confession.

A very different kind of attraction in *Frenchtown Summer* is Eugene's crush on Sister Angela, who came to town one summer to teach piano at the convent. Eager to take piano lessons from her, Eugene describes "plunging into agonies of longing" and being "dumb with desire" at her closeness beside him on the piano bench (52). He dreams of holding her hand and kissing her lips, only to find her mysteriously gone at the end of the summer.

These kinds of fantasies are part of any boy's adolescence, but Cormier's memories are vivid, and he has captured their painful and sometimes dangerous sweetness in the characters of Eric, Paul, and Eugene. Teachers may be reluctant to approach the subject of teenage sexual fantasy as classroom discussion, but the author's delicate handling of the subject in his novels may at least reassure readers that they are not alone in their feelings and that those feelings are normal. Teachers who do feel comfortable with the topic may approach writing assignments or discussion through such questions as these:

- How are the characters of Eric, Paul, and Eugene similar in their feelings about love?

- What do their feelings reveal about them as young men?

- How might "teenage crushes" be necessary to future healthy male-female relationships?

- In what way(s) might sexual attraction to older women be dangerous?

Murder and Forgiveness

Another incident in the memoir that recalls other Cormier characters and echoes a disturbing theme occurs when Eugene proudly wears his aviator helmet and goggles, "striding through the streets / like a World War hero," and the town bully, Hector Henault, snatches the helmet from Eugene's head, smashing the goggles underfoot. Holding back tears, Eugene says silently, "Die, you dirty rat, die," imitating James Cagney, whom he remembers seeing in the movies. Three days later Henault is crushed by the wheels of a truck, and Eugene tells us, "They said he died instantly. / I was awestruck / by my power to kill" (12–13). Cormier was fascinated by the struggle between good and evil and the gray area that sometimes exists between guilt and innocence. We find this theme manifested also in the schizophrenic Ozzie of *Fade*, who, because he is periodically invisible, finds he can kill at will and never suffer the consequences. And he sees no wrong in it. Similarly, Jason of *The Rag and Bone Shop* consciously decides to commit murder just to make sense of his confession to a crime he did not commit. And Cormier even turns this theme on its head in the case of Eric Poole of *Tenderness*, a sociopathic killer who is released from jail by masterfully manipulating the law, only to be later charged with the murder of a girl he was actually trying to save from drowning. The irony is chilling when we learn that Cormier set out in this book to create a murderer with whom readers would sympathize in the end. Cormier is expert at presenting us with dilemmas that test our moral ethics or values, and students might find it challenging to examine his works with questions like these:

* Does Ozzie's mental illness in *Fade* excuse him from the killing he does?

* Can we attribute Jason's desire to kill Bobo Kelton in *The Rag and Bone Shop* to the psychological abuse he suffered at the hands of Trent, the interrogator? Is Jason responsible for his decision to kill, or can we blame his murderous intentions on Trent?

* In *Tenderness*, Eric Poole is charged with killing Lori Cranston, though he was actually trying to save her from drowning. Does the fact that he is a serial killer make up for the injustice of this charge and his possible execution?

Closely related to the struggle between guilt and innocence in Cormier's books is the struggle for redemption. In *Frenchtown Summer*, Eugene recalls going to confession and being given a penance of ten Our Fathers and ten Hail Marys. Still, he wonders if the sin of touching himself, to which he never confesses, destroys his state of grace and dooms him to the fires of Hell. His fear is echoed in the character of Larry LaSalle in *Heroes*, who does so much good for the town, but ends up raping young Nicole Renard, ruining her life forever and driving Francis to thoughts of murdering him in desperation. When Francis angrily confronts Larry, saying, "You were our hero, even before you went to war. You made us better than we were . . ." Larry replies, "Does that one sin of mine wipe away all the good things?" (Cormier 1998, 115). Haven't we all wondered as much at some time in our lives? Our students might certainly benefit from the opportunity to discuss this question further.

The Demon Inside

"You are what you do" (2001b, 68). Trent the interrogator's wife said this to him the night before she died. He took it as an indictment, and it stayed with him long after her death. Forcing confessions from innocent suspects is nothing to be proud of, and Trent is guilt-ridden by the callousness and coldness he exhibits while questioning these suspects. He is especially disturbed by his interrogation of twelve-year-old Jason Dorrant, yet he never gives in to the nagging voice inside that tells him to ease up, that the boy is innocent. He knows this without a doubt, yet he pursues the confession unflinchingly. Trent's tactics are similar to those of Brint, the interrogator of Adam Farmer in Cormier's (1977) *I Am the Cheese*. In fact, the author has admitted that they are more or less the same person. But we never get inside Brint's mind as we do Trent's, so we never know whether he is conflicted about his unyielding questioning of the young boy. Still, closely examining the similarities between the two makes for interesting discussion. Students might discuss or write about these questions:

- In what ways are Brint and Trent similar in their approach to the interrogations of Adam in *I Am the Cheese* and Jason in *The Rag and Bone Shop*? In what ways do they differ?

- How does Brint's motivation in questioning Adam differ from Trent's motivation in questioning Jason?

- How do Adam and Jason react to their interrogators? How do their reactions affect their interrogators?

- What do the questioning styles of Brint and Trent reveal about their character?

Though it manifests itself in a different manner, the idea that "you are what you do" brings to mind Archie Costello's words to his stooge

Obie at the end of *Beyond the Chocolate War* (Cormier 1985). When Obie blames Archie for all the terrible events that have happened at Trinity High School and for ruining so many lives, Archie tells him:

> Oh, I'm an easy scapegoat, Obie. For you and everybody else at Trinity. Always have been. But you had free choice, buddy. Just like Brother Andrew always says in Religion. Free choice, Obie, and you did the choosing. . . . Don't feel bad, Obie . . . you've just joined the human race. . . . You'll always have me wherever you go and whatever you do. Tomorrow, ten years from now. Know why, Obie? Because I'm you. I'm all the things you hide inside you. That's me. (264)

And again in *The Chocolate War* we see Goober, Jerry Renault's best friend, trying to convince Jerry to sell the chocolates and worrying that something terrible will happen to Jerry if he doesn't give in, yet he watches and does nothing in the end when Jerry is savagely beaten by the bully Emile Janza. Was Goober really helpless to intervene? Is he truly a friend? "You are what you do."

In his many speeches to teachers and students, Robert Cormier often admitted that *he* is Archie Costello—and all the other characters who do awful things in his books—revealing his almost compulsive desire to understand the good and bad in himself through the characters he created. Encouraging students to explore this theme of duplicity in Cormier's works may help them better understand its manifestation in themselves and others. Realizing that there is good and bad in everyone and focusing on one of Cormier's favorite quotes, "Evil will prevail when good people do nothing," can be a profound experience for young readers who are themselves often struggling with confusing desires and temptations.

The Summer of the Airplane

Robert Cormier ends *Frenchtown Summer* with a touching anecdote about Eugene and his father. Eugene swears he saw an airplane in a neighbor's backyard—a World War II plane just like those he had read about. His brother and friends scoff at his story at first, but then are convinced to follow him back to where he saw the plane. They find only a yard full of weeds. Pitied and laughed at by the older boys, Eugene withdraws into the shadows, glad to be alone and unseen as families gather outside the tenements, trying to catch the evening breeze. Then his father, smoking a cigarette and speaking to no one in particular, muses, "Funny thing. / I saw an airplane this morning / on the way to the shop, / in the backyard of the three-deckers / on Fifth Street . . . But it was gone / when I looked again / on the way home . . . Eugene saw it, too" (111). All was right in Eugene's world once again—and perhaps, for a while, in Robert Cormier's world as well.

Robert Cormier's Major Works

1960	*Now and at the Hour*
1963	*A Little Raw on Monday Mornings*
1965	*Take Me Where the Good Times Are*
1974	*The Chocolate War*
1977	*I Am the Cheese*
1979	*After the First Death*
1980	*8 Plus 1* (anthology of Cormier's short stories)
1983	*The Bumblebee Flies Anyway*
1985	*Beyond the Chocolate War*
1988	*Fade*
1990	*Other Bells for Us to Ring*
1991	*I Have Words to Spend* (collection of Cormier's newspaper and magazine columns, edited by Connie Cormier)
1991	*We All Fall Down*
1992	*Tunes for Bears to Dance To*
1995	*In the Middle of the Night*
1997	*Tenderness*
1998	*Heroes*
1999	*Frenchtown Summer*
2001	*The Rag and Bone Shop*

Books

Bott, C. J. 2004. *The Bully in the Book and in the Classroom*. Lanham, MD: Rowman and Littlefield.

Bushman, John H., and Kay Parks Haas. 2005. *Using Young Adult Literature in the English Classroom*. New York: Prentice Hall.

Campbell, Patricia J. 1989. *Presenting Robert Cormier*, updated edition. Boston: Twayne.

———. 2006. *Robert Cormier: Daring to Disturb the Universe*. New York: Bantam Doubleday Dell.

Cline, Ruth, and William McBride. 1983. *A Guide to Literature for Young Adults*. Chicago: Scott Foresman.

Donelson, Kenneth L., and Alleen Pace Nilsen. 2005. *Literature for Today's Young Adults*, 7th ed. Boston: Pearson.

Herz, Sarah K., and Donald R. Gallo. 2005. *From Hinton to Hamlet*, 2d ed. Westport, CT: Greenwood.

Hyde, Margaret O. 2005. *Robert Cormier*. New York: Chelsea House.

Kaywell, Joan F., ed. 1993. *Adolescent Literature as a Complement to the Classics*, Vol. 1. Norwood, MA: Christopher-Gordon.

Monseau, Virginia R. 1996. *Responding to Young Adult Literature*. Portsmouth, NH: Boynton/Cook–Heinemann.

Monseau, Virginia R., ed. 2004. *A Curriculum of Peace: Selected Essays from English Journal*. Urbana, IL: NCTE.

Monseau, Virginia R., and Gary M. Salvner, eds. 2000. *Reading Their World: The Young Adult Novel in the Classroom,* 2d ed. Portsmouth, NH: Boynton/Cook–Heinemann.

Moore, John Noell. 1997. *Interpreting Young Adult Literature.* Portsmouth, NH: Heinemann.

Pennac, Daniel. 1999. *Better Than Life.* Portland, ME: Stenhouse.

Pipkin, Gloria, and ReLeah Cossett Lent. 2002. *At the Schoolhouse Gate: Lessons in Intellectual Freedom.* Portsmouth, NH: Heinemann.

Probst, Robert E. 2004. *Response and Analysis: Teaching Literature in Secondary School,* 2d ed. Portsmouth, NH: Heinemann.

Reid, Louann, ed. 1999. *Rationales for Teaching Young Adult Literature.* Portsmouth, NH: Heinemann.

Rosenblatt, Louise M. 1995. *Literature as Exploration.* New York: Modern Language Association.

Stover, Lois Thomas. 1996. *Young Adult Literature: The Heart of the Middle School Curriculum.* Portsmouth, NH: Boynton/Cook–Heinemann.

Stringer, Sharon A. 1997. *Conflict and Connection: The Psychology of Young Adult Literature.* Portsmouth, NH: Boynton/Cook– Heinemann.

Book Chapters

Bushman, Kay Parks, and John H. Bushman. 1993. "Dealing with the Abuse of Power in *1984* and *The Chocolate War.*" In *Adolescent Literature as a Complement to the Classics,* Vol. 1, ed. Joan F. Kaywell, 215–22. Norwood, MA: Christopher-Gordon.

Campbell, Patricia J. 1997. "Robert Cormier." In *Writers for Young Adults,* Vol. 1, ed. Ted Hipple, 291–301. New York: Scribner's.

Cormier, Robert. 1992. "A Book Is Not a House: The Human Side of Censorship." In *Authors' Insights: Turning Teenagers into Readers and Writers,* ed. Donald R. Gallo, 65–74. Portsmouth, NH: Boynton/Cook–Heinemann.

Samuels, Barbara G. 1993. "The Beast Within: Using and Abusing Power in *Lord of the Flies, The Chocolate War,* and Other Readings." In *Adolescent Literature as a Complement to the Classics,* Vol. 1., ed. Joan F. Kaywell, 195–214. Norwood, MA: Christopher-Gordon.

Articles

Bugniazet, Judith. 1985. "A Telephone Interview with Robert Cormier." *The ALAN Review* 12 (2): 14–18.

Campbell, Patty. 2001. "The Last Cormier." *Horn Book* 77 (5): 623. Retrieved 9 Nov. 2003: http://search.epnet.com/direct.asp?an=5210163&db=aph.

Cormier, Robert. 1985. "The Pleasures and Pains of Writing a Sequel." *The ALAN Review* 12 (2): 1–3.

———. 2001. "A Character by Any Other Name . . . ." *English Journal* 90 (3): 31–32.

Ellis, W. Geiger. 1985. "Cormier and the Pessimistic View." *The ALAN Review* 12 (2): 10–12, 52.

Gallo, Donald R. 1984. "Reality and Responsibility: The Continuing Controversy Over Robert Cormier's Books for Young Adults." *Voice of Youth Advocates* (Dec.): 245.

Monseau, Virginia R. 1991. "Cormier's Heroines: Strength Overlooked." *The ALAN Review* 19 (1): 40–41, 43.

———. 1994. "Studying Cormier's Protagonists: Achieving Power Through Young Adult Literature." *The ALAN Review* 22 (1): 31–33.

Myers, Mitzi. 2000. " 'No Safe Place to Run To': An Interview with Robert Cormier." *The Lion and the Unicorn* 24: 445–64.

Nodelman, Perry. 1983. "Robert Cormier Does a Number." *Children's Literature in Education* (Summer): 94–103.

Schwartz, Tony. 1979. "Teen-Agers' Laureate." *Newsweek* (16 July): 87–88, 92.

Silvey, Anita. 1985. "An Interview with Robert Cormier." *The Horn Book* (May–June): 289–96.

Snodgrass, Mary Ellen. 1988. "Teacher's Guide to *After the First Death*." Jacksonville, IL: Perma-Bound.

Stringer, Sharon. 1994. "The Psychological Changes of Adolescence: A Test of Character." *The ALAN Review* 22 (1): 27–29.

Film Adaptations

The Bumblebee Flies Anyway. 1999. Dir. Martin Duffy. Perf. Elijah Wood,
    Rachael Leigh Cook, Janeane Garofalo, Joe Perrino. USA
    Entertainment.
The Chocolate War. 1988. Dir. Keith Gordon. Perf. Ilan Mitchell Smith, John
    Glover, Wally Ward. MCEG.
I Am the Cheese. 1983. Dir. Robert Jiras. Perf. Robert MacNaughton, Hope
    Lange, Don Murray, Robert Wagner, Cynthia Nixon. Almi Pictures.
A Little Tenderness. Forthcoming. Dir. John Polson. Perf. Russell Crowe.
    Green Street.

CD-ROM

"Rationales for Challenged Books." 1998. NCTE/IRA.

Bott, C. J. 2004. *The Bully in the Book and in the Classroom.* Lanham, MD: Rowman and Littlefield.

Campbell, Patricia J. 1989. *Presenting Robert Cormier,* updated edition. Boston: Twayne.

———. 2001. "The Last Cormier." *Horn Book* 77 (5): 623. Retrieved 9 Nov. 2003: http://search.epnet.com/direct.asp?an=5210163&db=aph.

———. 2006. *Robert Cormier: Daring to Disturb the Universe.* New York: Bantam Doubleday Dell.

Cline, Ruth, and William McBride. 1983. *A Guide to Literature for Young Adults.* Chicago: Scott, Foresman.

Cormier, Robert. 1974. *The Chocolate War.* New York: Pantheon.

———. 1977. *I Am the Cheese.* New York: Pantheon.

———. 1979. *After the First Death.* New York: Pantheon.

———. 1984. "In the Heat." In *Sixteen Short Stories by Outstanding Writers for Young Adults,* ed. Donald R. Gallo, 154–52. New York: Dell.

———. 1985. *Beyond the Chocolate War.* New York: Knopf.

———. 1988. *Fade.* New York: Delacorte.

———. 1992. *Tunes for Bears to Dance To.* New York: Delacorte.

———. 1997. *Tenderness.* New York: Delacorte.

———. 1998. *Heroes.* New York: Delacorte.

———. 1999. *Frenchtown Summer.* New York: Random House.

———. 2001a. "A Character by Any Other Name. . . ." *English Journal* 90 (3): 31–32.

———. 2001b. *The Rag and Bone Shop.* New York: Delacorte.

Duncan, Lois. 1980. "Breaking the Rules." *The ALAN Review* 7 (3): 1.

Fleischman, Paul. 1988. *Joyful Noise*. New York: HarperTrophy.

Headley, Kathy Neal. 1994. "Duel at High Noon: A Replay of Cormier's Works." *The ALAN Review* 21 (2): 1–5.

Myers, Mitzi. 2000. " 'No Safe Place to Run To': An Interview with Robert Cormier." *The Lion and the Unicorn* 24: 445–64.

Nauman, April D. 1999. "Re-Reading the Bad Guys." *Teaching for a Tolerant World, Grades K–6*, ed. Judith P. Robertson, 107–20. Urbana, IL: NCTE.

Pipkin, Gloria, and ReLeah Cossett Lent. 2002. *At the Schoolhouse Gate: Lessons in Intellectual Freedom*. Portsmouth, NH: Heinemann.

Rationales for Challenged Books. 1998. CD-ROM. Urbana, IL, and Newark, DE: NCTE/IRA.

Reid, Louann. 1999. *Rationales for Teaching Young Adult Literature*. Portsmouth, NH: Heinemann.

Snodgrass, Mary Ellen. 1988. "Teacher's Guide to After the First Death." Jacksonville, IL: Perma-Bound.

Stringer, Sharon. 1994. "The Psychological Changes of Adolescence: A Test of Character." *The ALAN Review* 22 (1): 27–29.